The Developing Child

Recent decades have witnessed unprecedented advances in research on human development. Each book in The Developing Child series reflects the importance of this research as a resource for enhancing children's well-being. It is the purpose of the series to make this resource available to that increasingly large number of people who are responsible for raising a new generation. We hope that these books will provide rich and useful information for parents, educators, child-care professionals, students of developmental psychology, and all others concerned with childhood.

Jerome Bruner, University of Oxford
Michael Cole, Rockefeller University
Barbara Lloyd, University of Sussex
Series Editors

The Developing Child Series

Learning
Disabilities
A Psychological
Perspective

Sylvia Farnham-Diggory

Harvard University Press
Cambridge, Massachusetts

Copyright © 1978 by Sylvia Farnham-Diggory
All rights reserved
Printed in the United States of America
Second printing 1979
Library of Congress Cataloging in Publication Data
Farnham-Diggory, Sylvia.
    Learning disabilities.

    (The Developing child)
    Bibliography: p.
    Includes index.
    1. Learning disabilities.   I.   Title.
II.   Series.
RJ506.L4F37   618.9′28′588   78-5514
ISBN 0-674-51921-3
ISBN 0-674-51922-1 pbk.

Dedication

Some years ago I was collecting data in a school on the edge of a large city. It was not a glamorous school. The teachers who had been assigned to it did not want to be there. Education for the disadvantaged had not yet become a national priority, so no federal money was pouring in. The general atmosphere was one of deterioration, discouragement, and apathy.

I had been working out of a first-grade classroom taught by a woman not far from retirement. I took children individually from this classroom to an experimental room that had been set up down the hall where we played some word games. The children had become accustomed to seeing me return to the classroom with a child by the hand and knew this meant I was ready for another child. Hands flew desperately and strenuously into the air. Everyone would have a turn, but no one wanted to wait. The teacher was tolerant. Any interruption in the dull day's work was as welcome to her as to the children.

Knowing I was waiting for her to select the next child, the teacher pointed to the back of the classroom. A row of children sat there. I don't remember that their hands were raised. "Take one of those," the teacher said. "Those are the dregs at the bottom of the barrel. And don't bother to bring them back." I looked, stricken, at the faces of those children, six-year-olds.

I cannot write about this even now without fighting back tears, but in truth the children did not seem especially affected. Their world was full of adult cruelty. This was nothing new. The children in question (I learned later) were waiting to be tested and eventually removed to special classes. Under the laws of that state (now changed) they could not be tested until they were eight years of age. In the meantime, they sat in first grade, waiting.

The teacher, of course, knew her words should not have been spoken. At the end of the school day, as we watched the children march out of the building, she burst into tears. And through her sobs I glimpsed the ravages of chronic failure—day after day, year after year, staring at the uncomprehending faces of children who cannot learn.

If we are going to rescue the back-row children, we must find out what is really wrong with them. We must develop diagnostic and remedial procedures that have a scientific basis. Until we do, both teacher and child will be condemned to a mainstream of despair.

Long ago I made a silent vow to the back-row children, *and* to their teacher: I cannot help your generation, but I will try to help the next ones.

This book is meant as partial payment of those dues.

Acknowledgments

I thank the following publishers for permission to quote from their copyrighted material: Reidel Publishing Company, copyright 1974, N. Geschwind's *Selected Papers on Language and the Brain*; Van Nostrand Reinhold Co., copyright 1977, H. Ginsburg's *Children's Arithmetic*; and John Wiley & Sons, Inc., copyright 1976, D. M. Ross and S. A. Ross, *Hyperactivity*.

Early work on this book was carried out during my tenure as a Fellow of the National Institute of Education, in the Spring and Summer of 1976. However, no official support or endorsement by the National Institute of Education is intended or should be inferred.

On a personal basis, I would like to thank my colleagues at the NIE for a highly stimulating fellowship.

I would also like to thank my colleagues at the University of Delaware for their encouragement, and for their friendly tolerance of my obsession with writing.

Finally, the book would never have been possible without the patience, protection, and fierce secretarial skills of Cathi Hollenbeck.

S.F.D.

Contents

Learning Disabilities

Reeling and Writing . . . and then the different branches of Arithmetic—Ambition, Distraction, Uglification, and Derision . . . Mystery, ancient and modern, with Seaography . . . Drawling, Stretching, and Fainting in Coils . . . Laughing and Grief.

—Lewis Carroll

1 / Compass Points

The concept of *learning disabilities* is mysterious and complex. If you have a learning-disabled child, or know of one, if you are a teacher of learning-disabled children, or if you are merely interested in the topic professionally or otherwise—you must accept one fundamental fact: The field has not yet been reliably charted. The best any surveyor can do is to stake out some potentially revealing domains.

In my first four chapters, I have staked out the historical domain. The ideas found there—those of Hinshelwood, Orton, Werner, and others—still form the basis of much educational diagnosis and practice. If you have a learning-disabled child in a special program, you may be surprised to hear that the rationale behind his curriculum is probably forty or fifty years old, going on one hundred. This does not mean his program is a bad one, but it does mean the program is not based on current scientific theory in the areas of human learning and thinking.

Educational practice separated from psychology in the 1930s, through no fault of its own. For the past several decades, psychology has been engaged in an exploration of radical behaviorism—an exploration that declined about fifteen years ago, with the onset of cognitive psychology (or, as it is sometimes called, information-processing psychology). Radical behaviorism was not relevant to human learning ability or disability, so it could not provide the scientific support that educational practice needed. Cognitive psychology, however, has the supports—the technology, the concepts, and the intellectual leadership—that education needs. More and more educators are becoming aware of this, and are updating their psychological background. More

1

and more cognitive scientists are becoming aware of the urgent need for their research findings. Some of these findings are described in Chapters 9 through 12—a section of the book that charts where I think we will be going, scientifically, in the analysis and treatment of learning disabilities.

The middle section—Chapters 5 through 8—is descriptive of the current scene. We will look at test data, protocols, case histories, and experimental data—in an effort to understand what the term *learning disabilities* now refers to. Readers who are allergic to history can begin with Chapter 5, but the leap is not recommended. Historical flagstones, in this case at least, provide the surest footing into the future.

THE PROBLEM OF DEFINITION

The field currently called learning disabilities includes notions of brain damage, hyperactivity, mild forms of retardation, social-emotional adjustment, language difficulties, subtle forms of deafness, perceptual problems, motor clumsiness, and, above all, reading disorders—almost the entire field of special education. As you can imagine, this has led to a number of problems. There is no simple way of categorizing all the phenomena of special education and, therefore, no simple way of categorizing learning disabilities. Arguments over what learning disabilities *really* are have taken the flavor of a Gilbert and Sullivan melee, as exemplified by Edward Fry's "do-it-yourself terminology generator" shown in (1). The generator is supposed to be a joke, but the sober truth is that it works.

The explosive development of the field springs primarily from the fact that the term *learning disability* sidesteps the stigmata and hopelessness generally associated with such terms as *retardation, brain damage*, or just plain *slow*. Many parents would rather believe that a child suffers from a defect like "perceptual dysfunction," which sounds as if it can be corrected at least as well as astigmatism can be. Hence there is now a tendency to call every kind of school problem a learning disability.[1]

This overinclusiveness will eventually diminish, but in the meantime it has certain political advantages. The parents who are boarding the learning-disabilities bandwagon are forcing communities to pay attention to educational problems they

DIRECTIONS: Select any word from Column 1. Add any word from Column 2, then add any word from Column 3. If you don't like the result, try again. It will mean about the same thing.

1 Qualifier	2 Area of Involvement	3 Problem
Minimal	Brain	Disfunction
Mild	Cerebral	Damage
Minor	Neurological	Disorder
Chronic	Neurologic	Dis Synchronization
Diffuse	C.N.S.	Handicap
Specific	Language	Disability
Primary	Reading	Retardation
Disorganized	Perceptual	Impairment
Organic	Impulse	Pathology
Clumsy	Behavior	Syndrome

The above system will yield 1,000 terms but if that is not enough you could use specific dyslexia, aphasoid, neurophrenia, or developmental lag. (C.N.S. = Central Nervous System.)

1. Fry's do-it-yourself terminology generator. *From Frye (1968). Copyright 1968 International Reading Association. Reprinted by permission.*

might otherwise evade. These parents are, for the most part, intelligent and well-educated, and they have established the National Association for Children with Learning Disabilities, an organization with branches in many states which has considerable political clout. One measure of this is the insertion into the Education for All Handicapped Children Act (U.S. Public Law 94-142) a special provision for children with "specific learning disabilities."[2] The provision makes a definition mandatory.

The United States Congress has accepted the following definition of learning-disabled children:

> Those children who have a disorder in one or more of the basic
> psychological processes involved in understanding or in using
> language, spoken or written, which disorder may manifest itself
> in imperfect ability to listen, think, speak, read, write, spell, or
> do mathematical calculations. Such disorders include such condi-
> tions as perceptual handicaps, brain injury, minimal brain dys-
> function, dyslexia, and developmental aphasia. Such term does
> not include children who have learning problems which are pri-
> marily the result of visual, hearing, or motor handicaps, or men-
> tal retardation, of emotional disturbance, or environmental, cul-
> tural, or economic disadvantage. [Section 5(b)]

Publishing this definition has amounted to waving a red flag in
front of a herd of bulls—parents and professionals alike. Far
from clarifying the situation, the definition inspired so much
snorting and ground-pawing that the conceptual dust has grown
thicker than ever. Part of the problem arises from the fact that
we lose sight of what a definition is for. Definitions are not truth:
they merely set up the conditions under which particular actions
are to be taken. Some of those actions may be experiments.
Some of the experiments may produce results that have bearing
on truth. But the definitions themselves simply name the game.

Congress needs to name the game of moving federal tax dol-
lars into communities for the support of children who have special educational needs. Federal funds are already available for
children with visual, hearing, or motor handicaps, mental retardation, emotional disturbances, and environmental disadvan-
tages. Such children are therefore excluded now, and the children
targeted by the new Act can be labeled by whatever terms have
flowed from any particular community's terminology generator.
As William Cruickshank wrote:

> If a child happens to live in the State of Michigan, educators refer
> to him as a perceptually disabled child. If the child is a resident of
> California, his education may be provided if he is classified as an
> educationally handicapped or neurologically handicapped child.
> In Bucks County, Pennsylvania, he will be placed in a class for
> children with language disorders. If he moves from California to
> New York State, he will change from an educationally handicap-
> ped child to a brain injured child. On the other hand, if he moves
> from Michigan to Montgomery County, Maryland, he will stop

being a perceptually disabled child and become a child with specific learning disabilities.[3]

No one has any certainty about what is really wrong with these children. But whatever it is, let us find *some* name that will include them in the broadest possible beam of federal help. Arguments about definitions boil down to that simple pragmatic requirement.

FINDING THE CHILDREN

A number of operational problems have arisen. Because we do not know what learning disabilities really are, and because they seem to include the entire field of special education, we have not been able to devise legally unambiguous modes of diagnostic testing. In the absence of specific knowledge, educators traditionally fall back upon normative ideals. A learning-disabled child is presumably not up to a "grade level" that can be specified in terms of achievement-test scores. Grade-level work is what 50 percent of the children in a particular grade are doing. Since schools routinely collect achievement data, a child can be unambiguously identified with reference to grade-level norms in reading and other subjects.

But if a child is, say, two grade levels below the norm in reading, does that mean he is learning-disabled? He may just be what one school headmaster called "all round poor." We should, then, compare his achievement to his potential, to a measure of his basic intelligence. Again, we do not know exactly what intelligence is, but we can get a norm-referenced measure of it—a score on a standardized IQ test. A popular test for these purposes is the Wechsler Intelligence Scale for Children (WISC), which includes both verbal and nonverbal sections. The so-called performance IQ is derived from such tasks as matching block designs. The verbal IQ includes, for example, vocabulary knowledge. The full-scale IQ is derived from the combined verbal and performance scores.

From the standpoint of federal lawmakers, educators ought to be able to put together some formulaic brew of achievement-test scores, intelligence-test scores, age, and grade level which will clearly designate a particular child as learning-disabled and, therefore, as a proper beneficiary of special federal assistance. In practice, however, this makes about as much sense as adding up all the different leaves in a forest, dividing by the number of plants, subtracting the days since the last rainfall, and multiplying by the density of the shrubbery—in order to predict the growth rate of a particular dandelion. There has to be a better way. And indeed federal amendments are continually being proposed, revised, postponed, and rejected in an attempt to find one. In the meantime, Congress is using a rule of thumb: the states are permitted to designate 12 percent of all children aged five through seventeen as handicapped (this is an empirically derived number and reflects the actual incidence). The states are further permitted to designate one sixth of these 12 percent as learning-disabled, by any diagnostic means they choose. Whatever learning disability is, then, it is 2 percent of *something*.

Statistical incidence of learning disabilities. The figure 2 percent was not pulled out of a hat. In 1970, the National Center for Educational Statistics (a branch of the U.S. Office of Education) conducted a survey of approximately 2,000 public elementary and secondary school principals. The sample was stratified to represent the nation's 81,000 public schools. Principals of the 2,000 schools filled out a questionnaire on the number of their students with specific learning disabilities—*based on the above definition*—and the reported result was 2.6 percent.[4] When the sampled schools were separated into low- versus high-income areas, the estimate separated into 3.5 percent and 2.0 percent.

Although this must be considered the official count, there are many other estimates in the published literature. A 1973 summary is shown in (2).[5] As you can see, these "unofficial" estimates are much higher than 2 percent.

THE PROBLEM BEFORE US

We are faced, then, with a mystery of extensive practical importance. Something unknown is wrong with the learning capabilities of a substantial proportion of our citizenry. We will not know exactly what to do about this until we understand exactly what is wrong—and this makes the mystery a scientific one. The

Source	Definition and nature of sample	Estimate (%)
Eisenberg (1966)	Sixth graders who were reading two or more years below grade level; large metropolitan city	28
HEW Nat'l. Advisory Committee on Dyslexia and Related Reading Disorders (1969)	Varied; a wide range of geographic locations	15
Myzklebust and Boshes (1969)	Four-year study of 3rd and 4th grade children in Chicago suburbs	7.5−15
Rubin and Balow (1971)	967 1st, 2nd, and 3rd graders who were part of a medical research project in the Minneapolis-St. Paul area	24−41

2. *Minskoff's (1973) summary of reports on the incidence of learning disabilities.*

science needed for the job is to be found somewhere in the domain of cognitive psychology. Because it is a new field, many of the data are unfamiliar to teachers, clinical psychologists, physicians, neurologists, opthalmologists, school psychologists, and others concerned with the diagnosis and management of learning-disabled children. Conversely, many of the phenomena of learning disabilities are unknown to the scientists who can supply valuable research insights. One purpose of this book is to bring the two domains closer together—by providing practitioners with information about the nature of the science that can help them, and by providing scientists with information about the practical world of learning disability.

I will begin with a review of the early research on learning problems. There are two historical lines to be considered. One, originating with Alfred Strauss in the mid-1940s, included an emphasis on emotional lability and hyperactivity, as well as on perceptual disorganization. The second line, which included the work of Samuel Orton in the 1920s, began earlier and centered on dyslexia.

After this I will examine the current scene: Who are the learning-disabled children, as we now see them? What is dyslexia? What is arithmetic disability? What is hyperactivity?

Then I will explore the theoretical framework of information-processing psychology, which may hold the key to future breakthroughs. We do not yet know what all those breakthroughs will include, but we do know something about where they will occur. One might say that at least we have a map of the ballpark. In the course of examining basic theory and research, new ways of thinking about diagnosis and treatment will also become evident.

The overall objective of this book is to introduce to the reader a new set of analytical guidelines. Whether you are the parent of a learning-disabled child, a special educator, a student teacher, a researcher, or merely an interested bystander, it will be necessary for you to think critically about this strange field called learning disabilities. And by the time you have finished this book, you will, I hope, have some new resources for doing so.

2/ Early Views of the Brain-Injured Child

Most writers begin their history of learning disabilities with the publication of Kurt Goldstein's book, *Aftereffects of Brain Injuries in War*, in 1942.[1] The book is cited because of the influence it had on Alfred Strauss, a neuropsychiatrist who was a refugee from Nazi Germany. Goldstein's general theme was that, even after the brain wounds healed, behavioral disturbances persisted. The implication, for Strauss, was that comparable disturbances in children's behavior could be attributed to brain injuries.

Strictly speaking, this inference was not a logical one, but it had two important consequences: it encouraged research into subtle forms of brain injury and into unsuspected causal mechanisms (anesthesia during the birth process, for example); and it helped disturbed children and their parents climb off the painful hooks of self-blame. Until the concept of brain injury was introduced, children who behaved badly and failed in school were considered to be somebody's fault. But an accident to the brain was nobody's fault: one could stop feeling guilty and set about seeking help.

From his base at the Wayne County Training School in Michigan, Strauss wrote a very influential book with Laura Lehtinen called *Psychopathology and Education of the Brain-Injured Child*, published in 1947.[2] It is important to realize that this book was about exceptional children. Such children, like mentally normal children, show wide individual differences in behavior. In trying to develop appropriate educational strategies, Strauss and Lehtinen grouped exceptional behavior into six categories. One category was of special interest, so-called exogenous brain damage: something external to the genetic developmental plan was responsible for the damage. Exogenous children were described as emotionally unstable, perceptually disordered, impulsive, distractible, and repetitive. This was behavior that Goldstein had also observed in his brain-injured soldiers. In children, it later became known as the *Strauss syndrome*.

There were two other influences affecting the Straussian characterization of a brain-injured child. One was the then current notion regarding equipotentiality of brain function. This term was introduced by Karl Lashley in 1929 and referred to the likelihood that one part of the brain could substitute for another.[3] Lashley showed that rats will become learning-disabled if one takes out chunks of their brains. However, the *location* of the extirpated chunk did not seem to matter; what mattered was the *size* of the chunk. The implication for Strauss was that it was not necessary to specify the location of brain damage in children in order to assert that brain damage had occurred. This was a curious bit of theoretical illogic, and another followed. Strauss seems to have concluded that because nonspecific brain injury could be shown to result in behavioral disorders, then behavioral disorders could imply nonspecific brain injury. He apparently believed that brain damage "was frequently the result of small, diffuse hemorrhages scattered throughout the brain."[4]

We now know that such neurological theorizing was a confused oversimplification. More sophisticated research in brain physiology has shown that specific localization of function does exist. Lashley had been studying only one type of learning behavior in only one type of animal, and his instruments were crude by modern standards. With better instruments, different animals, and more complex learning tasks, brain researchers showed that removal of small bits of the brain in particular locations *would* have different effects on learning behavior. Clinical neurologists had long since observed similar differences in patients who suffered localized brain injuries. In 1964, an influential psychologist-pediatrician, Herbert Birch, published a collection of research and clinical papers supporting the modern neurological position: "Brain damage may vary with respect to etiology, extent, type of lesion, locus, duration of damage, rate at which the damage has been sustained, time of life, and developmental stage at which the injury has occurred."[5] The behavior resulting from these variances might be quite different. Note that

Birch was not telling us to drop the concept of brain injury, only to become more knowledgeable about what it really meant.

WERNER'S CONTRIBUTION

Besides Lashley, another theorist had an important influence on Strauss. This was Heinz Werner, a Gestalt psychologist who, like Strauss, was a refugee from Nazi Germany. Werner shared with other Gestalt theorists a conviction that learning and development produced a restructuring of the mind. Werner was particularly interested in the process of *differentiation*, a term borrowed from biology. It referred, for example, to such embryological phenomena as the budding of fingers from the stub of a hand. Once the differentiation process was complete, a functional *integration* had to take place—through practice, the fingers had to become able to work together. The complementary processes of differentiation and integration characterized many forms of biological growth, and Werner believed them to characterize mental growth as well. Note how compatible this notion is with that of brain equipotentiality. In effect, Werner thought mental development began with an equipotentiality of the mind. Gradually, specific capacities differentiated out of the mental mass. Once formed, the capacities had to be integrated, and mental coordinations could take place. As presented in his remarkable book *The Comparative Psychology of Mental Development*, Werner believed he saw these principles in many forms of development—animals, children, primitive man, and psychopathological man.[6]

For example, with reference to the development of number concepts, Werner believed that the process began with the "natural number space" of the hand. He noted similarities between children who counted on their fingers and primitive men who counted on theirs, and also found it significant that finger agnosia (inability to tell, with your eyes closed, which finger was tapped) was associated with arithmetic disabilities. (A case history of a child displaying finger agnosia is reported in Chapter 7.) The next step in the differentiation of the number schema was "dominantly optical in nature." Werner was not sure how this transition occurred, but cited such examples as "children will frequently pick up the objects they are counting and still later only point to them; finally only a glance is necessary." In this glance, presumably, important mental developments are taking place. "Only those pupils who have developed . . . methods for dealing with optical numerical forms are able to deal with abstract number concepts."[7]

On the basis of such theorizing and experimentation, Werner and his colleagues developed curricula. A good example of the results can be found in "Principles and Methods of Teaching Arithmetic to Mentally Retarded Children" by Doris Carrison (a teacher) and Werner, published in 1943.[8] The program incorporated Werner's views that development normally moved from tactile-kinesthetic forms of expression and representation, through the visual, to the abstract. Applications to arithmetic learning were straightforward. Children first worked with large materials (such as pegboards) which actively involved their whole bodies. They were then transferred to smaller devices, which reduced motor involvement but did not eliminate it. Always the materials presented salient visual patterns. Eventually the numerical ideas would lose their dependency upon spatial, concrete properties and emerge as true abstractions.

Werner's interest in perception had a strong influence on Strauss, and subsequently on the field of learning disabilities. The quality of Werner's theorizing is illustrated by his 1944 article, "Development of Visuo-Motor Performance on the Marble-Board Test in Mentally Retarded Children."[9] The marble boards were 11-inch squares, each containing 10 rows of 10 holes each. Two boards were used. The experimenter (out of the child's sight) made a pattern of red and black marbles on one board. The pattern was then shown to the child who copied it on his own board. The experimenter used a scoring system which noted the sequence of the child's moves as well as his accuracy. The particular patterns are shown in (3).

On the basis of the sequential data, Werner carried out a higher-order analysis of what he called *configurational organization*. As could be predicted from his general developmental theory, Werner looked for an integration of clearly articulated (differentiated) parts. "The child copies, for instance, Pattern II by building first one square, then the other. Such performance presupposes obviously that the child recognized the two subforms with respect to each other and to the whole."

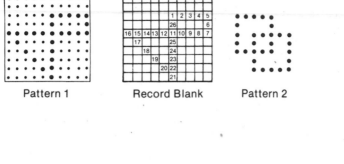

Pattern 1   Record Blank   Pattern 2

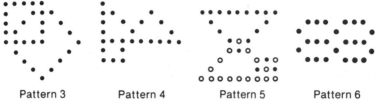

Pattern 3   Pattern 4   Pattern 5   Pattern 6

3. *The six patterns of the marble-board test. From Werner (1944). Copyright 1944 by The Journal Press. Reprinted by permission.*

Deficient performances were characterized by too much attention to the whole or by too much attention to the parts. Both of these conditions indicated a less mature level of activity. Still more primitive was a strictly *linear* performance, where the child was guided by lines and apparently did not perceive the form-characteristics of the patterns at all. The four types of configurational organization are shown in (4).

THE STRAUSS SYNDROME

The hyperactivity and distractibility of brain-injured children were of great concern to Strauss. In their paper on disorders of conceptual thinking, Strauss and Werner summarized the general behaviors which they believed to characterize brain-injured children.[10]

1. *Forced responsiveness to stimuli*—Any noise, movement, or object immediately captured the child's attention. Goldstein

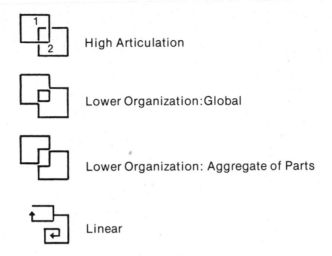

High Articulation

Lower Organization:Global

Lower Organization: Aggregate of Parts

Linear

4. *Types of configurational organization (Pattern 2). From Werner (1944). Copyright 1944 by The Journal Press. Reprinted by permission.*

earlier had seen similar behaviors in brain-damaged adults, and called the phenomenon *stimulus bonding.* The term reflected his observation that a passing stimulus seemed to compel the patient's attention. This was quite different from distractibility motivated by boredom.

2. *Pathological fixation*—Brain-injured children were thought to be perseverative in nature. Once they began a simple task like bead stringing, for example, they continued it much longer than a normal child would. That seemed to contradict the distractibility characteristic, but it may have been part of the same system. The child perseverated because the stimulus continued to capture his attention. Probably it continued to seem new to him.

3. *Disinhibition*—Excessive motor activity resulted in the type of behavior we now refer to as *hyperactivity.* Strauss thought that brain-damaged children were especially attentive to stimulus features that elicited motor activities. The "bounciness" of a round object, for example, might be especially salient to the child. (I once knew a child who could never be trusted with pencils. The "jabbiness" of a sharp pencil point was more than he could resist.)

4. *Dissociation*—This referred to Werner's concept of integration. The brain-injured child was believed unable to comprehend a pattern as a whole. Instead, he would aggregate parts, as shown in (4). The integration failure manifested itself in a variety of activities. Generally, the child was disorganized in almost everything he did.

These characteristics led Strauss and Lehtinen to design a learning environment for brain-injured children which was quite different from a traditional classroom. The special environment decreased the stimulation impinging on the child. Walls were left plain, windows were covered, even the child's study materials were cut out of the distracting context of illustrated workbooks and mounted on plain paper. Often the child worked in a screened area that insulated him from the sight and sound of others.

There have been many direct descendants of that early period —William Cruickshank and Newell Kephart, for example.[11] But the significance of the Strauss-Werner contribution lies primarily in its general influence. Every current worker in the field of learning disabilities can trace some piece of personal theory or methodology back to Strauss and his collaborators at the Wayne County Training School.

3/ Structural Approaches to Dyslexia

Reading difficulties are far and away the most crucial component of any learning-disability syndrome. Most children with other learning problems (say, arithmetic problems) also have reading and spelling problems. If we can understand what the reading disorders are all about, we will have solved a large proportion of the learning-disability puzzle. For this reason, the history of reading disorders is of special importance.

There are numerous ways of classifying and labeling reading disorders in the field of clinical neurology alone—and even more ways in the field of reading instruction. Understandably, people who favor one classification argue that the other classifications are wrong. Thus some people have argued against the term *dyslexia* on grounds that it is a catch-all, and that more accurate terms exist (such as "reading delay"). As I pointed out in Chapter 1, these are arguments about truth, and we cannot settle them. We do not yet know what dyslexia is, and it is therefore futile to try to invent a definition that will amount to an explanation. Someday, when we have an explanation, we may need a new term. In the meantime, *dyslexia*—which is indeed a catch-all term, as are such work-horse terms as *cancer, schizophrenia,* and *cerebral palsy*—will serve.

In 1968, dyslexia was defined as follows by the Interdisciplinary Committee on Reading Problems: "A disorder of children, who despite conventional classroom experience, fail to attain the language skills of reading, writing, and spelling commensurate with their intellectual abilities."[1] What definitions preceded this one?

The early historical period centered on the work of James Hinshelwood, a Scottish ophthalmologist with an interest in neurology; and the later period, on the work of Samuel Orton, an American neurologist. The two periods are characterized by an emphasis on *structural* aspects of the disorder—specific brain sites, hypothetical connections, and so forth—as against an emphasis on the *functional* aspects: how information gets from one part of the brain to another. Hinshelwood was the structuralist, Orton the functionalist.

HINSHELWOOD'S CONTRIBUTION

James Hinshelwood began publishing in 1895 on a mysterious affliction known as *acquired word-blindness,* sudden loss of the ability to read. His summary monograph, *Congenital Word-Blindness,* was published in 1917.[2] Hinshelwood had an explicit theory of the role of the brain in reading, and he tested it clinically. His theory was that there must be separate places in the brain for (a) visual memory of the general everyday type; (b) visual letter memory; and (c) visual word memory. If that were true, Hinshelwood said, then it should be possible to find pure cases of each. He set about collecting cases from his own practice and through contact with other physicians.

Visual mind-blindness. In 1896, Hinshelwood published a report of a tailor who was fired from his job because he had lost the ability to perform it.[3] Hinshelwood noted that many important aspects of visual memory are represented by tailoring skills. One must have a memory for shapes (patterns) and for how they fit together. "Even in simple stitching the visual memory comes into play and guides the complicated movements of hand and fingers." One must also remember where one's spools and scissors are kept. The tailor's fellow-workers were especially annoyed by the fact that he kept forgetting where he had put things and spent more time looking for them than sewing. The poor tailor also began to forget his way home.

But he could *perceive* things normally. Thus, Hinshelwood wrote, we must distinguish between a visual perceptual center and a visual memory center. "The accumulated riches of our life experiences . . . are stored up in a special cerebral area, the visual memory center . . . Derangements of this center are evidenced by the various forms of mind-blindness. The objects are distinctly seen, but they convey no information to the individual since they are no longer recognized by him [they can no longer activate memories]."[4]

Hinshelwood diagnosed the tailor as having localized brain damage brought on by alcoholism. He thought the locale was in the vicinity of the *angular gyri*. The exact location is not important at the moment; the point is that Hinshelwood believed the visual memory center of the everyday type to have been affected. True, the patient had also lost the ability to read, thus proving, Hinshelwood said, that word memory was a subsystem of general visual memory without being identical to it. Word-blindness is usually defined only in cases where general visual memory remains intact. Theoretically it must exist in the broader instance as well, and Hinshelwood offered his tailor as proof.

Visual word-blindness. The most common types of dyslexia are characterized by an inability to recognize words. The individual letters may be recognized quite well. Further, numbers are recognized equally well—and, more important, *groups* of numbers (1062 read as "one thousand and sixty-two") are recognized. Hinshelwood thought such facts indicated that there must be separate (but adjacent) memory centers for words, letters, and numbers. To prove this, he needed cases of pure word-blindness, and they came readily to hand. One of Hinshelwood's reports in 1898 concerned a man of fifty-three who lost the ability to read words after having a stroke. He could read letters, numbers, and groups of numbers fluently. He could also write to dictation and copy words correctly, but could not read what he had written. On the basis of this one symptom, Hinshelwood recognized that the man must have had a stroke. "I gave it as my opinion that the inability to read was not due to any ocular defect, but to a lesion in the visual word-memory centre situated in the *angular* and *supra-marginal gyri* on the left side of the brain and supplied by a branch of the Sylvian artery, that the lesion was a small hemorrhage or more probably thrombosis occluding that branch of the Sylvian artery supplying the centre."[5] Hinshelwood predicted that additional symptoms of stroke would appear, and they did. The patient developed paralysis and aphasia, and died in about nine weeks.

(The case incidentally illustrates the transient nature of certain symptoms of brain damage. Not only does the organic state change, but patients may rapidly learn to compensate functionally for initial difficulties, thereby obscuring the fact that the difficulties still exist. Clinical tests may thus suggest one conclusion early in the course of an affliction and another conclusion a short time later.)

THE DISCOVERY OF DEVELOPMENTAL DYSLEXIA

It was during this period that an important scientific notion dawned upon the medical literature: dyslexia might be present in some people from birth. Congenital dyslexia should, if it existed, produce many of the same symptoms as those produced by brain injury in adults. Could that be demonstrated? Were there children whose reading disorders matched those reported for adults in the clinical literature? We take the answer so much for granted now that we forget someone had first to think of it.

There is some dispute over who did in fact think of it first, probably because several people thought of it simultaneously. A school doctor by the name of James Kerr was awarded a prize by the Royal Statistical Society in 1896 for an essay on school hygiene which included reference to word-blindness in children.[6] But Hinshelwood preferred to attribute the discovery to a physician named Pringle Morgan, who said (in a letter that Hinshelwood later published) that *he* got the idea from a paper by *Hinshelwood* published in 1895.[7] Pringle Morgan said in this letter that he could find no reference to the possibility that the condition described by Hinshelwood might also be congenital. So Pringle Morgan sent in a note to the *British Medical Journal* on November 7, 1896, describing a fourteen-year-old boy who might be an instance of *congenital* word-blindness.[8] Hinshelwood promptly wrote a letter to the editor commending the good doctor, advising him to encourage the boy to keep working and drawing parallels between Pringle Morgan's boy and his *own* (adult) cases first described in 1895.[9]

Although Pringle Morgan (or Kerr) must be credited for the initial insight, Hinshelwood went on to do the scholarly work that had to be done. Pringle Morgan and Kerr were not heard from again. But Hinshelwood's book *Congenital Word-Blindness* has become a classic. Here is a case from it.

A boy, 12 years of age, was brought in March 1902 to the Glasgow Eye Infirmary by his mother, to see if there was anything wrong with his eyesight. The boy had been seven years at school, and there had been from the outset the greatest difficulty in teaching him to read. The boy should have been in Standard V, but was now, after seven years, only in Standard II, and he could not get out of it because of his reading. He had made no complaint whatever about his vision, but his mother had brought him to the Eye Infirmary in order to discover if his eyesight had anything to do with his difficulty. His mother stated that he was in every other respect a sharp and intelligent boy. He had no difficulty with arithmetic, and could keep up with the other scholars easily in this department. He was now working at compound addition. His mother said that the other boys laughed at him in class, and that when he became excited his reading was worse than ever. He concealed his defect for a time by learning his lesson by heart, so that when it came to be his turn and he got a few words at the beginning, he could repeat the lesson by heart. His auditory memory, therefore, was evidently very good. On examining him I found that his reading was very defective for a boy who had been seven years at school. He could rarely read by sight more than two or three words, but came to a standstill every second or third word, and was unable to proceed unless he were allowed to spell out the word aloud, thus appealing to his auditory memory, or to spell it silently with his lips, thus appealing to his memory of speech movements . . . The words he stuck at were chiefly polysyllables, but this was not always the case, as he often failed to recognise by sight even simple monosyllabic words. He spelt very well, and when asked to spell the words which he had failed to recognise by sight, he nearly always did so without any difficulty. He read all combinations of figures with the greatest fluency up to millions. I made him do several sums up to compound addition. All of these he did smartly and correctly. His mother informed me that he had a splendid memory and could learn things by heart very easily. I wrote to his schoolmaster for information about the boy. He replied that the lad had experienced throughout his whole career in the school the greatest difficulty in learning to read, which had kept him very much behind in his progress through the school. He was strong in arithmetic, good at spelling, and average in other subjects, including geography and history.

"I have never," said his master, "seen a case similar to this one in my twenty-five years' experience as a teacher. There is another boy in his class who is quite as poor a reader, but this other boy is all-round poor, showing no sign of smartness in anything."[10]

I have quoted this at length because it remains one of the best descriptions around of dyslexic behavior. The syndrome has certainly not changed since the turn of the century, and neither have our informal methods of diagnosing and describing it. A dyslexic child is essentially a child with a history similar to the one we have just read.

Visual letter-blindness. Hinshelwood believed that word memory was not a compound of letter memory, but was an entirely different sort of memory located in a different place. If this supposition were true, then it should be possible to find patients who could read whole words but who could not spell them out or read individual letters. Such cases would provide a very strong test of Hinshelwood's hypothesis. In 1899 he reported five of them, none being patients of his own. One was a man of twenty-four who was recovering from a form of spinal meningitis.

His visual symptoms were somewhat remarkable. There was no object-blindness . . . [but] when tested with words and letters it was evident that a peculiar condition was present. On testing him with letters it was found that he could neither read nor write a single letter of the alphabet except *T* which he generally recognized and always named *Tom* which was his own name. Nor could he point out any named letter except *T*. The inability to recognize them was the same with all sizes and forms of letters both written and printed. On testing him with words, however, in a large number of trials it was quite evident that he could read almost every word presented to him, even words of three or four syllables and very unfamiliar ones, while at the same time he was quite unable to name or point out a single letter of the word he just read. But words such as *stethoscope, telescope, electricity, infirmary,* and so forth, were read at once. The word *job* was read at once, but when the letters were arranged *obj* and he was asked to read them he could not name a single one. The contrast between the fluency with which he read the words and his inability to make anything out of the individual letters was very striking. Substantives he could make out much better than verbs and could read them with the greatest fluency. Slight intentional mistakes in spelling and even reversing letters were not observed by the patient who read the words just as if no alteration had been made and did not seem conscious of anything peculiar about the word. Numerals he recognized and named as far as 9 but not

beyond that, and only the Arabic numerals, and not the Roman
. . . He had been instructed to educate himself by learning the letters of the alphabet again. This was done but only with partial
success . . . While he failed with many of the letters he wrote
readily words beginning with the same letters . . . [Where] he
failed to write *p, r,* or *n* . . . he wrote quite readily *pot, Robert,
nail,* and so on.[11]

Although this patient was not followed after leaving the hos-
pital, certain other patients were. Their faculties, Hinshelwood
noted, did not return simultaneously. In one case, number memory returned first, then word memory, and finally letter memory. "I do not know of any more convincing proof which could
be brought forward to demonstrate that these different groups of
visual memories are deposited in distinct cerebral areas."[12]

Normal and Defective Reading.   Hinshelwood's theory of
dyslexia probably came before his theory of reading. His views
on proper reading instruction were also an outgrowth of his
clinical observations. They had a "back to basics" flavor in 1917
which should remind us of the cyclical nature of reading contro-
versies.

To understand clearly the nature of the [dyslexic] defect . . . we
must analyse a little more precisely the cerebral visual processes
concerned in the act of reading and consider the manner in which
an individual learns to read. The following remarks, of course,
apply to the old-fashioned methods of learning to read. Of the
twelve cases reported in this book all had been trained in this way
. . . The first stage in the old method is to store up in the visual
memory the individual letters of the alphabet. When we have
stored [them] . . . we can recall them into consciousness at will
. . . It is by comparison with these permanent visual images of the
letters and words stored in this cerebral centre that we are able to
recognise the printed letters and words on the page of the book. If
this cerebral area is destroyed by disease, then the individual
loses this power of recognition and becomes letter- and word-
blind . . . Under normal circumstances this first stage [of learning
to read] is accomplished with comparative ease and rapidity,
there being only twenty-six letters in our alphabet, or taking capital and small letters, fifty-two visual images in all to be acquired.
The memory of words is first registered in our auditory memory

centre situated in the *tempero-sphenoidal lobe* and of course inti-
mately connected with the visual memory centre, as all the cerebral centres involved in language are connected with one another.
We are able to spell the words before we are able to recognise
them by sight. When the individual has stored up in the centre in
his left *angular gyrus* the visual memories of the individual letters
of the alphabet, and in his auditory centre the spelling of the
words, he is then able to enter on the second stage of reading. He
is now able to read words by spelling them out loud letter by letter, and thus by appealing to his auditory memory, he gets the
proper words; or sometimes he may simply be seen to move his
lips, spelling silently each letter, and thus appealing to his memory of speech movements . . . or he may sometimes be seen trac-
ing the letters with his fingers on the table and thus appealing to
his writing centre. To reach the third or final stage in the art of
reading is a much more formidable task, and requires for its accomplishment a much longer period of time. This third stage con-
sists in the gradual acquirement and storage of the visual memories of words. When this is accomplished, the individual reads
not by analysing each word into its individual letters, but by
recognizing each word as a separate picture. The words then cease
to be for such an individual simply a combination of letters [in
the 1899 paper Hinshelwood called them *congeries* of letters, a
nice old word that means a collection of things merely heaped
together]. Each word is regarded rather as an ideogram, picture,
or symbol which suggests a particular idea. The individual now
recognises a word, just as he recognises a landscape or a familiar
face, by its general outline and form without resolving it into its
constitutent details. He has now learned to read by sight alone.
When he looks at the words on the printed page, he can now
interpret them by comparison with the visual word memories
stored in his *angular gyrus,* and there is no need for further ap-
peal, as before, to his auditory memory or [speech movement]
memory or writing centre. He has now successfully attained the
final stage in the art of reading, *viz.,* the power of reading by
sight alone.[13]

Hinshelwood went on to point out that there were degrees of
proficiency to be expected among normal readers. He thought
some of the variation could be attributed to practice, some to
inborn visual-memory endowment. But truly dyslexic readers
were of a different order. They had, first of all, difficulty mastering the first stage of reading. Only with great persistence could

they learn the letters of the alphabet. Even more difficulty was experienced in mastering the second stage of reading, but it could be done—provided the children had been taught phonetic rules. Dyslexics taught by "look and say methods" (Hinshelwood's term, and it was clearly an old one even then) would never make it to this second stage. But mastery at this level again took enormous effort. Mastery of the third stage was almost impossible. "There is thus manifest in [dyslexic] children such a striking contrast between the capacity of the auditory and the visual memories that it at once reveals a condition which is so abnormal that it can only be regarded as pathology . . . They have been unable like [normal] children to furnish their visual memory centre with the visual memories of words, and it is the great and persevering efforts which are necessary to repair this failure and to remedy this defect which makes their educational career so different from that of the ordinary child."[14]

Again I have quoted Hinshelwood at length on the subject of what reading is, as well as what dyslexia is. This type of theoretical speculation is still around in a variety of forms, and has not yet been replaced by theories that we are *sure* are better.

Hinshelwood may have been wrong in various neuroanatomical particulars, but he was probably correct in principle—more so than was recognized at the time. Hinshelwood was first of all a literate scholar, and he did his homework. He was familiar with neurological cases, such as the one reported by a French physician named Dejerine. It was from Dejerine that Hinshelwood got the idea that the *angular gyrus* region of the left hemisphere was a critical site, although he was wrong about why it was critical. The site is not a visual word storehouse. Instead, it is an association area where triple connections can be made among visual, auditory, and kinesthetic areas of the brain. The importance of this site for reading was illustrated in the case of Dejerine's patient.

Figure (5) is a schematization of the brain from the top down. The left field of vision (involving the left retinal areas of both eyes) is connected to the right side of the brain; the right field of vision (again, both eyes) is connected to the left side of the brain. In Dejerine's patient, autopsy showed that the left visual cortex had been destroyed by a stroke. Visual information coming in through the shaded tracts in the diagram was therefore no longer

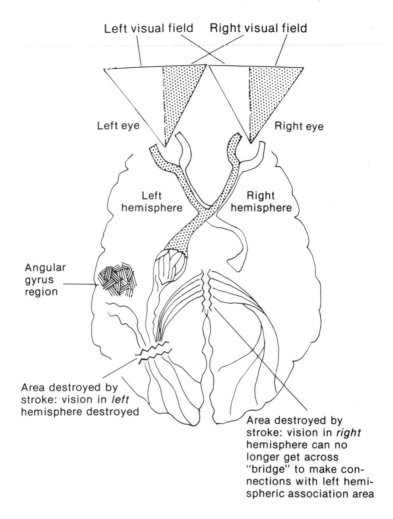

5. *Diagram showing the type of brain damage that can result in the loss of reading ability. If the patient cannot connect words that he sees right-hemispherically with the association area (angular gyrus) in the left hemisphere, then pure reading disability (without agraphia) will result. If, on the other hand, the angular gyrus is damaged, reading disability with agraphia will result. This is the more common condition—the patient cannot read, write, or spell.*

registered. Only the information coming in through the clear tracts, and going to the right hemisphere, was registered. Ordinarily such information could make contact with the left hemisphere by going across the *corpus callosum*—a bridge of fibers connecting the two hemispheres. But in Dejerine's patient that was no longer possible because the stroke had also damaged the *corpus callosum.*

Thus Dejerine's patient could *see* only with his right visual cortex. But what he saw—say, letters or words—could not be connected to the left *angular gyrus* region. None of this was known until after the patient died and an autopsy was performed. All that was known during the patient's lifetime after his stroke was that he had lost the ability to read—but only the ability to *read.* He could still write and spell, but could not read back what he himself had written and spelled correctly. After the autopsy, it was concluded that disconnection of the visual cortex from the *angular gyrus* region would produce this form of pure reading disability.

More commonly, however, this pattern of disconnection is not seen. Instead, a stroke may damage the *angular gyrus* region directly. In that case, the patient develops not only a reading disability but also a writing and spelling disability—known as *agraphia.*

It is important to note that such neurological theories are still viable today.[15]

4 / Functional Approaches to Dyslexia

In 1925 a paper appeared in the *Archives of Neurology and Psychiatry* entitled "Word-Blindness in School Children." The author was a physician who specialized in neurology, Samuel T. Orton, and the paper presented his new theory of dyslexia—one based on the notion of hemispheric imbalance.[1]

Orton believed that something was wrong with the brains of dyslexic children, but, unlike Hinshelwood, he thought the disorder to be functional in nature rather than structural. He found an important clue, he thought, in the mirror writing of certain children. In (6) we see an example taken from his 1937 book, *Reading, Writing, and Speech Problems in Children.*[2]

Orton believed that written productions were something like a print-out of information stored in the brain. Mirror writing therefore showed that the information must be stored in more than one orientation. It had been known for some time that the left hemisphere was responsible for the storage and production of language. Less was known about the functions of the right hemisphere, but Orton believed that they reflected the activities of the left. "The exact symmetrical relationship of the two hemispheres," he wrote in 1925, "would lead us to believe that the groups of cells irradiated by any visual stimulus in the right hemisphere are the exact mirrored counterpart of those in the left." Further, these mirrored images were remembered. The right hemisphere contained a mnemonic record, a reflected duplicate of information in the left hemisphere. These records could trigger matching motor activity. "The tendency common in young children to mirrored or reversed writing . . . points to the

.yss y 7eqef ⊕ 9radʃ biP s ₃ ₊ʃʃ₉ȣ

regood ed lʲ w qeʃ yM biₚ2 ₊ʃʃ₉ȣ

oⱨ g od ⱅ si qeʃ yʃʃ₉ȣ

The Easter Rabbit

The Easter Raddit keeps a very
Cheerful hen that likes to lay

S.T.O.-'36

6. *Writing of a left-handed boy. At the top is his spontaneous mirror-writing produced during his first year in school. Below is his product one year later when everything except the confusing b's and d's had been reoriented. From Orton (1937). Copyright 1937, Norton. Reprinted by permission.*

existence in the brain of a mnemonic record in mirrored form which serves as a pattern for these motor expressions."[3]

Learning to read and write correctly, then, was a matter of learning which hemispheric image to pay attention to. Normally a child learned that the left hemispheric renditions were the correct ones. In some cases, however, this learning did not develop normally. To understand what Orton thought went wrong, refer to (7). The figure is taken from Orton's 1925 paper and schematizes the distribution of certain types of cortical cells. The first, "visual perceptive," were the initial receivers of sensory information. Orton called that cortical level the "arrival platform." The next level up, "visual recognitive," contained brain cells that facilitated visual association of a limited type. Object recognition occurred at this level, but object *meaning* could occur only at the next level: "visual associative." In this area of the brain,

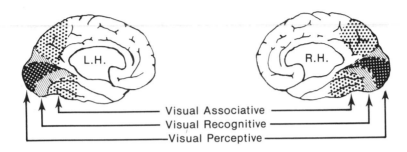

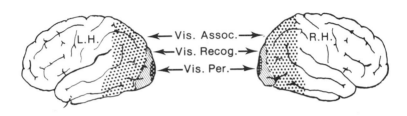

7. *Distribution of three types of cortical tissue. From Orton,* Archives of Neurology and Psychiatry, *1925,* 14, *582-615. Copyright 1925, American Medical Association. Reprinted by permission.*

connections could be made with other information from sensory and motor areas.

Orton believed that either hemisphere could effectively perform perceptive and recognitive activities, but that associative activities had to be performed by the left hemisphere alone. His evidence for that belief was straightforward, neurologically. Brain injury at the first and second levels did not impair behavior unless it occurred in both hemispheres. Simple perception and recognition could apparently be managed by whichever hemisphere remained intact. But third-level injury was a different story: damage to the right hemisphere made no difference, but damage to the left hemisphere produced word blindness. To Orton, this suggested "that the process of learning to read entails the elision from the focus of attention" of the right hemispheric images. When the left hemisphere was unable to perform that critical suppressive function, confusions and delays would result. There would be distortions of the motor output in both speech and writing, interference in the linking of visual symbols and sounds, and subsequent failure to associate sounds and meaning. Orton called the whole disaster *strephosymbolia*. The Greek roots of the term—*strepho* and *symbolon*—mean "twisted signs."

THE SYNDROMES OF STREPHOSYMBOLIA

Orton described six clusters of disabled behavior which he believed to represent dominance failure of the left hemisphere. These are briefly presented below. The syndromes still comprise what many consider the true domain of learning disabilities—as compared to the narrower domain of reading disability, so often emphasized by schools. Certainly these syndromes are included in the definition quoted in Chapter 1.[4]

1. *Developmental alexia*—unusual difficulty in learning to read, but no evidence of accompanying physical, mental, or emotional abnormality. There was normal auditory development and often a display of good intelligence and imagination in solving the problem of not being able to read. For example, the child might become very proficient at guessing the meaning of words and passages. Vision and visual-motor coordination skill in games like basketball were normal and often superior. As Orton pointed out, if you could not read road signs, you had to develop other ways of finding your way home. The reading disability took the form of letter confusion, letter reversals, word confusions and reversals, severe spelling difficulties, and often difficulties in writing.

2. *Developmental agraphia*—special difficulty in learning to write. This might accompany reading disability or exist by itself. Sometimes it took the form of extreme slowness in forming letters. In other cases, illegibility was the problem. Writing might be improved by a shift to the opposite hand or by a shift in direction—some agraphic children could do mirror writing as well (or as poorly) as normal writing. Or they could write with either hand. They might also be able to write better if they did not watch their hands.

3. *Developmental word deafness*—difficulty in recognizing the spoken word, delay and distortion of speech, but normal hearing. The child could understand environmental sounds quite well—car horns or dogs barking—but showed confusion in understanding words. Such a child might show a lack of attention to words because the words carried very little meaning. The word-deaf child in effect disregarded words, whereas normal children disregarded meaningless environmental sounds. Because verbal understanding was such an important component of intelligence, word-deaf children might appear retarded. Functionally, of course, they were, but their retardation resulted from a specific disability in processing language. Speech in these children was usually slow to develop. Verbal output showed distortion and confusion that reflected mishearings. For example, the child might say "pose" for "suppose," or "repeller" for "propeller," or "atween" for "between." Syntactical disorders might be present. The child might say "I have spoking." Generally, such children also developed reading and writing disorders.

4. *Developmental motor aphasia*—slow development and disorder of speech, but good understanding of the spoken word (that is, no word deafness). These children did not show an inattention to spoken language and usually tried very hard to express themselves. They recognized errors in their own speech and in the speech of others. Sometimes there was a speech defect, such as a lisp or a stutter. Once speech began to develop, it usually proceeded swiftly.

5. *True childhood stuttering*—spasms of the speech musculature which either blocked speech or produced mechanical repetitions. There might be overflow into other motoric systems— jerky movements of the arms, shoulder, or head. The disability might be present from the time the child first began to talk or not begin until middle childhood when the child was learning to read and write. Often writing disability coexisted with stuttering, and sometimes reading disability as well.

6. *Developmental apraxia*—abnormal clumsiness similar to the type of clumsiness exhibited by a right-handed person attempting to use his left hand. An apraxic child seemed to have "two left hands and two left feet," almost literally. There might be a delay in learning to walk, run, button clothes, tie shoes, handle spoons, skip, jump rope, ride tricycles. Speech muscles

and small hand muscles might also be affected. Hence, the apraxic child might also show speech and writing disorders.

Orton believed that all of these disorders resulted from confusions and conflicts at the associative level. The conflict was quite literally between the left and the right hemisphere. Normally no conflict developed because the left hemisphere controlled the operations of speech, writing, and reading. In the above syndromes, however, the left hemisphere was thought not to be in control.

REMEDIAL TRAINING FOR STREPHOSYMBOLIA

In the early thirties, Anna Gillingham and Bessie Stillman worked with Orton to develop a remedial program that reflected Orton's theory.[5] The emphasis was upon association deficiencies. A curriculum was designed to give afflicted children practice in linking kinesthetic, auditory, and visual information. The pedagogy reflected the learning theory of the period. The strength of a connection was assumed to be a direct function of the amount of practice. Drill-and-practice was therefore the order of the day—but it was enlightened. The child was given an informal explanation of his problem and of the pedagogical theory. He was, in other words, prepared for hard work. The following excerpt from a phonogram lesson unit is taken from the 1940 edition of the Gillingham and Stillman manual.[6]

> Each new phonogram is taught by the following processes which we refer to as Linkages, and which involve the association between the visual, auditory and kinesthetic [sensory systems] . . .
>
> *Linkage 1.* The card is exposed and the name and sound of the phonogram are clearly pronounced by the teacher and repeated by the pupil . . . It is here that most emphasis must be placed in case of a speech defect.
>
> *Linkage 2.* The letter is carefully made by the teacher and its form, orientation, etc. explained. It is then traced by the pupil over the teacher's lines, and copied, and written from memory, and written again with the eyes averted while the teacher watches closely.
>
> *Linkage 3.* The phonogram is shown and the pupil is asked to name it. Sometimes his hand is moved to form the symbol and he

is asked to name it without looking. The name of the phonogram must be associated with its "look" and "feel."

Linkage 4. The pupil writes the phonogram from dictation.

Linkage 5. The card is again exposed with the question, "What does this letter . . . say?" The same question is asked with the pupil's passive hand moved by the teacher to form the symbol while he looks away.

Linkage 6. The name of each phonogram is said by the teacher and the pupil gives the sound, e.g., "What does the letter *b* say?"
. . .

Linkage 7. The sound is made by the teacher and the name given by the pupil, "What is the letter (or phonogram) which says (b)?" . . .

Linkage 8. The sound is again made by the teacher and the symbol is written by the child, "Write the phonogram which says (b)." At times, this must be done with eyes averted. The letters should be named as the child's hand forms them.

. . . The authors would feel apologetic for the minute detail of presentation in this and the following chapters were it not for the repeated and insistent requests for full descriptions of procedure, pressed upon them even while they write.

The manual—into its seventh edition by 1970—was indeed detailed. The teacher was told exactly how to prepare materials. Daily lesson plans were provided. Typical error patterns were described and the teacher was shown how to get the pupil back on the right track. Sample pupil-teacher dialogues abounded.

It is not clear that Orton and his co-workers believed associative practice would produce left hemispheric dominance. The direction of causation was the other way around: dominance failures and struggles were responsible for the weak associations. Thus prosthetic linkages had to be formed through the Gillingham and Stillman drills.

Let me reiterate that the theoretical concepts we have reviewed in the historical chapters still form the basis of much current educational practice in the field of learning disabilities. J. Lee Wiederholt, who published a short history of learning disabilities in 1974, divided the historical sequence into three phases.[7] The *foundation phase* included the work we have been covering, that of Hinshelwood, Orton, and others. In the *transition phase*, at-

tempts were made to apply "foundation concepts," by developing diagnostic and remedial materials that were based on them.
The marble-board work of Werner, for example, has appeared
and reappeared in many different guises, as have the alphabetic
techniques recommended by Hinshelwood and the close-order
drills of Orton's collaborators. Finally, according to Wiederholt,
we have reached the *integration phase,* an eclectic approach to
the transitional materials based on the foundation concepts. In
fairness, some current work is looking toward more modern research, but most of what is taught in current courses on learning
disabilities amounts to a recapitulation of early neurological and
psychological theories. And, unfortunately, they have lost a
good deal in the recapitulations.

For that reason, I have taken you back to the fountainheads.
Strauss, Werner, Hinshelwood, and Orton described a domain
of behavior and remedial practice which is clearly observable
today in special classrooms for learning-disabled children. We
can take Orton's syndrome list as a field guide and classify all the
learning-disabled children we see. We can also classify remedial
pedagogy—it may be emphasizing the perceptual domain that
Werner favored, the connectivities that Orton favored, or the
minimal distractions that Strauss favored.

It is all still there, just as they said.

5 / Who Are the Learning-Disabled Children?

We have reviewed the historical beginnings of the answer to this question. Now we will examine current answers. To get an answer, of course, you must ask a question, and to ask a question objectively, you must use standardized questioning instruments —tests, interview formats, and so forth. Such instruments are far from perfect. Professionals who use them are often keenly aware of that fact. But what choice do they have? If someone—a school, a parent, a doctor—wants to know how intelligent a child is, what is the alternative to giving the child an intelligence test? If someone wants to know if the families of learning-disabled children differ in any way from the families of normal children, what is the alternative to using some kind of standardized interview technique? Modern descriptive data about learning-disabled children appear in certain forms—such as IQ averages, reading grade levels, and so forth—because those are the only forms available to the schools and to most clinical or counseling psychologists. (Newer ways of testing these children are not yet available, outside of a few specialized laboratories to be described later.) A monograph published by Freya Owen and her colleagues provides a good summary of data gathered by traditional psychometric instruments.[1]

Owen's study began with 76 children designated by the State of California guidelines as *educationally handicapped*, the state term for learning-disabled. Data were gathered on school achievement, IQ, drawing ability, handwriting ability, school adjustment, neurological development, speech development, parent and sibling data, and family atmosphere. A particular

35

value of the study is Owen's use of sibling comparison groups for both the learning-disabled sample and the matched controls.

Owen obtained her groups in the following way. The children in the school district—aged 5 to 15—who had been designated as needing remedial educational help (2 percent of the school population) were screened for those having a same-sex sibling. The normal school population was then canvassed in order to locate children of the same age and socioeconomic background as those in the learning-disabled sample. Normal children were included in the study only if they had siblings of the same age and sex as the siblings of the learning-disabled children. Parents of both sets of children (handicapped and normal) were also tested and interviewed.

AGE, SEX, AND SOCIAL CLASS

What were the demographic characteristics of the learning-disabled children? First of all, the majority of them (67 percent) were in the 8- through 11-year age range. Only 4 percent were 6-year-olds, and 10 percent were 7-year-olds. The remaining 18 percent of the learning-disabled children were in the 12- to 16-year-old age bracket. This is a typical distribution and comes about in the following way: young children (first and second graders) may be slow without being learning-disabled. Hence, teachers find it difficult to pinpoint learning-disabled children until the middle elementary grades. Older children with learning handicaps generally move into an academic program that does not tax their reading and writing capabilities. This is one reason why they disappear from the accounting charts. Another reason is that there are so few remedial specialists in high schools available to help them (or to keep count of them). What should not be concluded—in looking at the 67 percent as against the 18 percent figure—is that learning disability is less frequent in high school, or that it is cured by the time the disabled children get there.

Eighty percent of the children in Owen's learning-disabled sample were boys; 20 percent were girls. This is a typical sex distribution. In almost any sample of children with learning problems, 80 percent of them will turn out to be male. The reasons for this are unknown, but probably stem from the fact that males are more physically vulnerable than females. More male babies die in infancy, and those who live are outlived by females, on the average. The vulnerability is unquestionably genetic. It has been true for such a long time that our species has evolved a higher male birthrate, to compensate for the higher male deathrate.

Males are also slower to develop than females. In terms of developmental age, female babies are about a month more mature than males at birth, and the difference increases with age. A rule of thumb is that the growth rate of males is about 80 percent of the female rate, finishing up about two years later.

Would fewer boys suffer from learning disabilities if their schooling were delayed for a year or two? There is no simple answer to that question, because there is no simple relationship between physical development and learning abilities. All we can say at present is that a sex difference exists in the learning-disabled population, a fact that bears close watching.

To return to Owen's monograph, the socioeconomic background of her sample was indexed by the fathers' level of education. Sixty-three percent of the fathers had at least some college, and 21 percent had attended graduate school. Although this level of education is higher than the national average, it is not higher than average for the particular California community in question (Palo Alto). On the basis of their socioeconomic background (a potent predictor), the learning-disabled children in Owen's sample should have done quite well in school.

INTELLECTUAL ABILITIES AND SCHOOL PROGRESS

All of the children were given the WISC. The results are shown in (8). You can see that the learning-disabled children had a full-scale IQ (107) which was equivalent to the full-scale IQ of the normal comparison group (109). That was a deliberate match. But after the match was made, scores on the two parts of the IQ test—the verbal and performance scales—were examined separately. Here a difference appeared between the learning-disabled children and all the other children in the study. In the learning-disabled group, the score on the *performance* part of the WISC was higher than the score on the verbal part. In the other groups, the scores on both parts were about equal.

In (9) the subtest scores of the performance and verbal scales

	Full-scale IQ	Verbal scale	Performance scale
Learning-disabled	107	104	109
Siblings of the L-D group	107	106	107
Normal	109	109	109
Siblings of the normal group	113	113	113

8. *WISC intelligence test scores.* (*Data tabulated from Owen et al., 1971.*)

are graphed separately. You can see that the performance scores of the learning-disabled children were not only higher than their own verbal scores, but were actually higher than the performance scores of the normal children. It is this *unevenness* of WISC scoring that signals a psychometrician to be on the lookout for learning disability. However, it is very important to understand that the unevenness is merely a clue at the level of a clinical hunch. It is not a hard and fast statistical indicator. There are many normal individuals who are relatively good on the verbal scale of the WISC and poor on the performance scale, or vice-versa. That is exactly why the test was constructed in two sections—as an acknowledgment of the fact that intelligence is normally manifested in a variety of ways and that most people are not uniformly good on all of them.

A second important point is that we do not understand what the performance or verbal subtests are measuring. Psychologists and educators sometimes talk as if IQ tests were as scientifically accurate as a thermometer. They are not. They simply dip into some general problem-solving abilities—much like a bucket dipping into a flowing river. What is hauled up in the bucket is a very complex mixture. To understand that mixture scientifically, it has to be submitted to a variety of highly specialized analytical processes.

School achievement is often measured by the Wide Range Achievement Test (WRAT), developed by J. F. Jastak. The WRAT has several subtests. Owen and her group used only the word-reading and spelling subtests—since those scores correlate

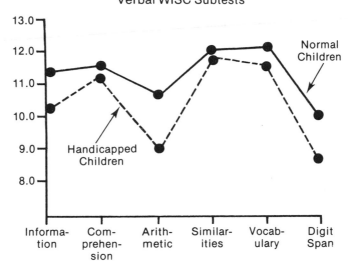

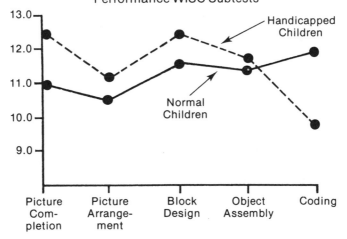

9. *Verbal and performance scales. Data from Owen, et al. (1971). Copyright 1971, Society for Research in Child Development. Reprinted by permission.*

with other measures of reading ability (such as comprehension) and with other school tasks. Scores on the WRAT can be converted to grade-placement scores.

The learning-disabled children were found to be about two grades behind their normal controls in reading ability and about a grade and a half behind them in spelling. The siblings of the learning-disabled children were about one grade behind the normal children in reading, and about half a grade behind in spelling. This is in spite of the fact that everybody had the same IQ. The grade-level lag became worse with age. Learning-disabled children in the higher grades had fallen even further behind their normal peers in reading and spelling.

The fact that the siblings of the learning-disabled children also showed reading and spelling problems suggested that some aspects of learning disabilities may run in families. Owen checked this further by giving parents the WRAT tests and also by examining their high-school grades in English. The parents of the learning-disabled children—especially the mothers—had poorer reading scores than parents of the normal children, and also had poorer high school grades in English. The former parents were mostly C students in those areas; the control parents were B students, on the average.

Handwriting samples were available from the spelling subtest of the WRAT. Learning-disabled children and their siblings showed handwriting impairments, relative to their controls. Their handwriting was irregular, weaved above and below the line, showed poor letter formation, letter reversals, and heavy or variable pencil pressure.

School adjustment was estimated from school records by raters who did not know anything else about the children—their WRAT scores, for example. Information in the records made it possible to categorize a child as ranging from excellent to very poor in school adjustment. The graph shown in (10) indicates that adjustment problems were more frequent among learning-disabled children and their siblings.

PERCEPTUAL-MOTOR AND SPEECH SKILLS

Ever since Werner's work, we have been concerned with the graphic abilities of learning-disabled children. In Owen's study, two kinds of drawing skills were assessed: the ability to draw a

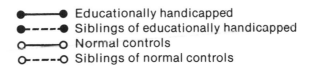

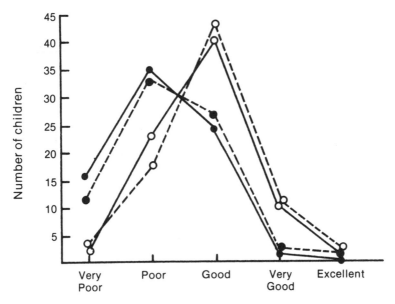

Teacher's judgments of school adjustment

10. *School adjustment. Data from Owen et al. (1971). Copyright 1971, Society for Research in Child Development. Reprinted by permission.*

human figure, as measured by the Draw-a-Person test, and the ability to copy geometric patterns, as measured by the Bender-Gestalt test. The important aspect of both tests is that their scoring systems have been standardized: data have been gathered on normal children of different ages. The performance of any individual child can thus be compared to the average for his age.

On the Draw-a-Person test, the child is free to draw any human figure. As many as 70 different items can be checked—whether the figure was given hair, correct number of fingers, and so forth. Generally, what is scored is the memory for detail and imagination. On the Bender-Gestalt test, the child copies geometric figures, some of which are quite complicated. The scoring system here includes errors of rotation and integration.

Both the learning-disabled children and their siblings were below average—and below their normal comparison groups—on these two tests of perceptual-motor functioning. The major problem on the Bender-Gestalt involved the *order* in which pattern components were copied. "The educationally handicapped children gave evidence over and over again that they were severely impaired in temporal order and in the ability to sequence events and objects appropriately. In our sample, we may conclude that the educationally handicapped child does not have a disability in visual perception: he has little difficulty in perceiving or matching; he has enormous difficulty in constructing or translating what he sees."[2] This kind of information is important with reference to the theory, presented in Chapter 12, of hemispheric functions. The left hemisphere is concerned with ordering and with sequential constructions. Ever since Orton, we have been mindful of the possibility that learning-disabled children may have weak left hemispheric skills. Owen's data are consistent with that proposition, as are data from other sources.

All of the children in Owen's sample were routinely evaluated for speech problems upon entering school. When she examined these data, Owen found that 47 percent of the learning-disabled children and 22 percent of their siblings had been referred for speech therapy. This compared to about 18 percent of the normal controls. The speech problems included articulation errors, expressive language difficulties, and receptive deficits. There were also more reports, by mothers of learning-disabled children, that one or both of their children had difficulty sitting and listening to stories. "Poor attention for stories in preschool educationally handicapped children," Owen speculated, "may well be precursors of later language disabilities."[3]

NEUROLOGICAL ASSESSMENT AND MEDICAL HISTORY

One might imagine tests of neurological capacity to be quite sophisticated, neurology being an older discipline than behavioral science. But, in point of fact, standard neurological examinations are relatively insensitive to all but the most severe forms of brain damage. For example, stand with your arms stretched out, close your eyes, and touch the tip of your right finger to your nose. If you miss your nose, you may have a problem. But practice a bit, and see how quickly your nose-finding skill develops. That is hardly a sensitive test of how well your brain works.

More modern neurological assessment batteries are beginning to include tests devised by psychologists. One, for example, involves the child's ability to recognize the equivalence between a tapped pattern, and a pattern of dots. The sounds "tap-tap, tap" would be represented by the dot pattern •• • as compared to the • •• pattern.[4] That particular test differentiated Owen's learning-disabled sample from the normal controls. So did another test invented by the same psychologist (Herbert Birch, whose remarks about brain damage were quoted in Chapter 2)—a test of left and right discrimination. Both the learning-disabled children and their siblings showed below-average discrimination. A more purely neurological test is one in which children are asked to imitate fast, alternating hand movement. Owen's learning-disabled children evidenced trouble with that one as well. All three of the above measures involve sequential abilities, but it is not clear what they involve neurologically.

Tests that did *not* discriminate between learning-disabled and normal children included measures of hand, foot, and eye preference, and walking on a balance beam.

Although extensive medical histories of the sample were apparently taken, details were not reported in the Owen monograph. We are told only that the following aspects of the medical records differentiated the learning-disabled from the normal groups: irritability during infancy, colic, poor listening skills after the age of two, temper tantrums, and mother-child conflicts. Apparently the learning-disabled children were suffering from some type of nervous tension from a very early age.

BRAIN WAVES

If learning-disabled children have subtle forms of brain-damage, we might expect them to exhibit abnormal brain-wave patterns. Brain waves are measured by electroencephalographic

(EEG) recordings. Small, highly sensitive electrodes are taped to the head, and the electrical activity they pick up is amplified and analyzed by various means—sometimes by just looking at the wave patterns, but more often by computer.

EEG technology has changed considerably in the ten years since the Owen data were collected. At that time, EEG data did not seem helpful. Eleven of Owen's learning-disabled children showed mildly abnormal EEG records, but then so did seventeen children in the various normal groups. Further, "In such records abnormality may be hard to judge because of the wide range of normal patterns in children and because criteria for abnormality are not too specific . . . In the majority of children EEG findings were not related to speech and language disorders, learning disorders, or to past medical histories. These are compelling reasons to state that at the present time the routine use of EEG is not useful in identifying familial patterns of learning disability."[5]

Ten years later, however, the situation has changed, primarily because of technological improvements in the recording and analysis of electrical activity of the brain. The field is now extremely complex, and the interested reader will have to pursue it elsewhere—for example, in the work of E. R. John.[6]

FAMILY ATTITUDES

In Owen's study, another question of great interest concerns the role of parents. Owen's parents were interviewed by professionals (psychologists or psychiatrists) who did not know which category the family was in—learning-disabled (child) or normal. Twenty-three 5-point scales were then constructed, so that the parents could be compared statistically. Thirteen of the dimensions concerned the parents' perceptions of their children; two concerned school; two, childrearing practices; four, parental attitudes; and two, overall family atmosphere.

How do you see your child? If there was a learning-disabled child in the family, parents perceived him as having perseverance problems both in school and out of it, as anxious, as having poor abilities in verbal (reading, spelling) and motor areas (clumsiness), and as having difficulty in controlling both his own impulses and his environment. These perceptions were all relative to the perceptions of parents who did not have a learning-disabled child.

Relative to siblings, learning-disabled children were perceived to have problems with anxiety, verbal abilities, impulse control, and general coping ability. However, the disabled children were thought to be better than their siblings in spatial knowledge. Unfortunately, it is not clear from Owen's monograph exactly what the parents were referring to in this case.

What do you think of your child's school? The scale for evaluating past schooling ranged from "school experiences have been happy and rewarding" to "school experiences have been unhappy, unsatisfactory, and sometimes extremely disturbing." The scale for current schooling ranged from "enthusiastic approval" to "extremely critical." On both measures, the parents of learning-disabled children were more negative than the parents of normal children—despite the fact that a special program (Owen's) for learning-disabled children was available in the district. The parents of learning-disabled children also felt the child's school experiences had been less satisfactory than those of a sibling.

Do you love your child? The question was not asked in such a way, but the interview data were examined for answers to it. Owen's conclusions were that "the only relationship found for the educationally-handicapped children and not for any other group indicated that, for these children only, mothers tended to withhold affection if the child was irresponsible and if he was disorganized [and he was often perceived to be disorganized, compared to his sibling]. Their siblings tended to receive more affection if they had higher verbal ability, persevered in school tasks, and if they were less worrisome to their mothers." About the fathers, Owen reports that "educationally-handicapped children certainly lived in a different world from their siblings in their relations with their fathers. They tended to lose the affection of their fathers if they were apathetic or worried, lacked concentration, or could not control their impulses, whereas the fathers did not seem to be affected by these same traits in the siblings."[7]

Do you push your child in school? The scale in this case ranged from "mild pressure on child for academic achievement" to "extreme pressure evidenced in unrealistic demands; early and continuing emphasis on academic learning; forcing child to do extra school work at home; punishing for failure." Mothers of learning-disabled children tended to put more pressure on them than they put on the siblings, but mothers of *control* children showed the same tendencies. Since everyone's siblings were younger, on the average, the trend probably signified the well-documented fact that mothers expect more of earlier-born children.

When correlations were examined, it was found that a relationship existed between pressure and anxiety, in both the learning-disabled and control groups. That is, the more anxiety expressed by the mothers, the more they revealed tendencies to press their children toward school achievement. Mothers were more likely to press normal children, including the siblings of the learning-disabled children, if they perceived their children to be verbally skilled and well-organized. This pattern, logically enough, did not appear in the learning-disabled group.

Academic pressure from fathers appeared to be related to their views of the learning-disabled child's perseverance and ability to carry responsibility. In the case of their siblings, fathers put on pressure in relation not only to perseverance but also to the child's general sociability and enthusiasm.

In other words, the parents of learning-disabled children—like the parents of normal children—are concerned over school progress, but recognize that their expressions of concern must be tempered by their children's characteristics and competencies. There is no shred of evidence that parents *produce* learning-disabled children through inappropriate academic pressures. This is not to say that conflicts between parents and teachers may not exist, as will be illustrated in the next chapter.

Is your family emotionally stable and well-organized? If it includes a learning-disabled child, the answer is likely to be negative—relative to families without such children. Learning disability is a disorganizing, emotionally upsetting factor, just as a physical disability would be. Maintaining a harmonious family atmosphere is difficult under the best of circumstances. If the family is prone to learning disabilities (in parents or in children), then the task is bound to be harder.

In this chapter I have sketched the best current descriptions we have of the characteristics of learning-disabled children. Most of the data have come from Owen's study, published in 1971, and not much additional new information has become available since that time—using traditional psychometric instruments.

As studied by such methods, learning-disabled children are shown to be in the eight- to eleven-year-old age range, predominantly male, of middle-class background with relatively well-educated parents. Their IQ is normal, but their reading, writing, drawing and spelling abilities run at least two years behind those of normal children of the same age. They may have speech problems and other indications of neurological dysfunction. Their school adjustment has been troubled. Their families have been affected by the stress of dealing with them, but since other members of their families—siblings and one or more parents—have also shown signs of similar difficulties, it would be unrealistic to attribute family problems to the learning-disabled child alone.

Depending upon the assessment criteria, from 2 to 40 percent of the school children in this country are believed to fit this general description (2).

6/ Four Dyslexic Children

In the concern over definitions, screening formulas, and group characteristics, the learning-disabled child himself may be lost in a theoretical shuffle. His problems as an individual are intricate; they extend far beyond our technical capacities to quantify them. He is part of a family that may or may not help him handle his problem intelligently and compassionately. He is part of a school system which may or may not know how to handle him *or* his parents. He may or may not have emotional resources of his own; he may or may not have a personal attitude of intelligent objectivity. He may—fortunately or unfortunately—be provided with psychiatric attention, or not, depending upon circumstance.

In this chapter, I will review some excerpts from case files of four dyslexic boys. Each of the children will be introduced through a sample of his own creative writing. We will then look at the story behind the stories.

THE CASE OF JACK

In (11), (12), and (13) we have three stories from Jack on his favorite topic: snakes. The stories are shown in his own handwriting, with his reading tutor's transcription below. We can see that this nine-year-old has built up a fund of information on snakes (despite his reading handicap) and shows imagination and humor.

Jack's file began about a year ago, when Mr. and Mrs. Smith brought him to the reading clinic. To quote from the initial clinic interview, "They think he has a problem in reading because he

48

The Rattler

a rattle snakes are poisos. If you are Biten you have little chang. dieing. The rattler, Copperheads and mocasin is, and Coral snake are poisonous. The rattler venm is yelbw

The Rattler

A rattle snakes are poisonous. If you are bitten you have little chance
dying. The rattler, copperheads and moccasins, and coral snake are
poisonous. The rattler venom is yellow.

11. Jack's Story 1.

doesn't seem to comprehend what he is reading, nor can he adequately remember what is read to him. They have him read
aloud, and he stumbles over many high-frequency words and
often substitutes words which make no sense in context." Testing at the clinic confirmed the reading, spelling, and comprehension problems that were described.

From the notes concerning early development, we read that
Mrs. Smith had one miscarriage before her pregnancy with Jack.
To carry Jack, she needed hormone injections each month because her body did not manufacture enough amniotic fluid. Her
health was poor during the pregnancy because of a gall-bladder
problem. Jack was born postmaturely with a relatively short
labor of two hours. Birth was natural, with no instrument or
drugs. He weighed just under six pounds and was described as a
jittery newborn with nervous tremors.

The grass Snake

Once apon ed a Time
I was cutting the gras.
I stoped to enpery the
Bag on the lenon morer
when I enperd it a littel
green snqke Fall out oF the
Bqg. it Fall on the
ground. It started to
slether oFF in the
gras. I ran aFter the
snqke. I callit and
pited it up. it was a
grds snake.

The Grass Snake

Once upon a time I was cutting the grass. I stopped to empty the bag on the lawn mower. When I emptied it a little green snake fell out of the bag. It fell on the ground. It started to slither off in the grass. I ran after the snake. I caught it and picked it up. It was a grass snake.

12. *Jack's Story 2.*

Jack's early development seemed normal, even accelerated. He was sitting up at four months, creeping at seven months, and beginning to talk before he was ten months old. He was walking at the age of a year. However, he had a great many allergies, and especially violent reactions to bee stings. He had many high fevers as a baby, chronic tonsillitis, and a tonsillectomy was performed when he was eighteen months old. At the age of two, he hit his head on a piece of furniture, cutting himself to the extent that stitches and later plastic surgery were required.

At the age of six, Jack may have been poisoned by cyanide gas. One night he came downstairs to tell his parents that he was not feeling well. His parents smelled smoke and rushed upstairs. A foam pillow had been ignited by a night light. It had been smoldering, giving off cyanide gas, for several hours before bursting into flames. Neurological testing found no abnormalities, but for several months thereafter Jack was on phenobarbitol.

Other aspects of Jack's development seemed to have been normal. He was good at sports, bicycle riding, and especially swimming. Apparently he began swimming as a toddler. His parents felt that he had no problems with fine motor coordinations such as writing or cutting, but it is stated in his records that he did not especially enjoy cutting or coloring.

There were no reported parental stresses. Jack's parents are in their early thirties and have had high-school educations. The father went on to get technical training and works for a plastics firm. The mother is a receptionist. They seem to have a stable marriage and are very concerned about Jack.

Jack's first year of school seemed quite normal. The teacher in first grade was described as fairly demanding, but Jack was nevertheless in the top reading group. The "whole word approach" to reading was used at that level. Second grade was a very bad year, however. Jack actually could not read, although apparently he had a good memory for the whole words taught in first grade, and so went on to the low reading group in second grade. Now, behavior problems began to appear. Jack's emotions were subject to sudden changes, and he avoided friends. His parents wanted him held back in second grade, but the school pushed him on to third grade with the provision that he get extra help from the resource teacher. He was tested psychologically at that time. His IQ was in the low-average range on the verbal section of the WISC and in the high-average range on the performance section. His full-scale IQ was 99. Since there were no evident retardation problems, Jack was promoted to third grade, and then to fourth.

In fourth grade, Jack had different teachers for reading, English, social studies, and science. His report card listed his effort

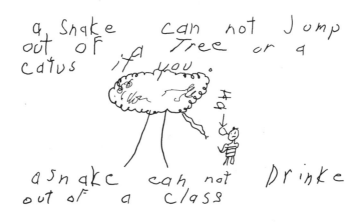

Wath A Snake Can't Do

a Snake can not Jump
out of a Tree or a
catus if you.

a Snake can not Drinke
out of a class

What a Snake Can't Do

A snake can not jump out of a tree or a cactus at you.
A snake can not drink out of a glass.

as moderate in reading and consistent in the other areas. Although it was reported that he was working very hard, his parents felt that his placement in several "slow" sections did not present a challenge to him. He was, however, unable to read the materials required for science and social studies, so his parents read them to him. He was often unable to retain the information adequately.

Notes about a school conference revealed the extent to which Jack's social studies teacher, Mrs. Brown, viewed the problem as one of family interference in schoolwork rather than one of learning disability (and possible brain damage). Mrs. Brown felt that Jack's mother was researching and writing his projects for him. As a consequence, Jack was said to fidget and waste time in class during the free period for working on projects. During her last conference with Mrs. Smith, Mrs. Brown said she tactfully

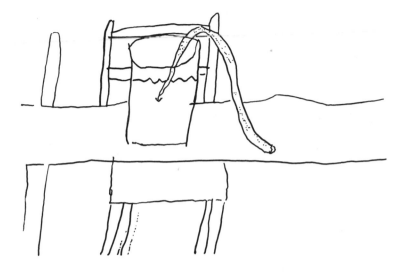

(snake drinking out of a glass)

13. *Jack's Story 3.*

tried to bring out the fact that doing Jack's work for him was doing him more harm than good. But according to Mrs. Brown the result of this conference was far from satisfactory. Jack came in the very next day and proceeded to copy some of his mother's work that she had given him to bring in, so that he would have something to do during the free period.

When asked how Jack has been doing on tests and in class assignments, Mrs. Brown replied that he did all right, usually averaging about 80 percent on quizzes and tests. She also commented that she naturally did not expect as much from Jack and graded him accordingly. For instance, she would not mark off for his grammar and spelling errors. Also she said that, while she would refuse to correct another child's work if he copied answers straight out of the book, she would accept such work from Jack. In fact, she would even be pleased with such work as long as Jack found the information for himself.

Jack's file also included notes that explained what kind of work he and his mother did together. When asked if either she or Mr. Smith helped Jack with his homework, Mrs. Smith readily replied that she did, every night. She then went on to explain how one of Jack's teachers assigned extensive long-term projects, involving both research techniques and concepts that Mrs. Smith considered to be far too advanced for fourth grade students. Because she felt Jack could not even begin to complete these assignments on his own, they did them together. Mrs. Smith described their two-to-three-hour nightly sessions as follows. First she read out loud, next she explained to Jack what she had read, and last she wrote down the answers to the specific questions asked on a project guide. The clinician who was interviewing the parent then made some recommendations to the effect that it would be better for Jack to dictate the answers to his mother, rather than for her to teach them to him by rote. However, a second school conference three months later indicated that the problem had continued. Mrs. Brown began the conference by relating how she was perturbed by the fact that Jack's parents still did his work for him. She said that Jack continued to fidget and waste time in class when she gave the children a free period to work on their projects. Her position at this point was that she had simply given up on Jack. For example, she had given him a high grade in effort last marking period just so she would not have to "face another conference" with the parents. Also she said that she had deliberately begun to ignore Jack's attention-getting behavior about a month ago. At the same time, she stopped giving him special help with in-class assignments. She felt that Jack now "hated" her. Nevertheless, she said, she planned to continue treating Jack in this manner because "somebody has to put their foot down and teach this boy that he cannot always have his own way." She added that she hoped the reading clinic would instruct Jack in a group rather than on a one-to-one tutoring basis, because having the full attention of one teacher at the clinic tended to "spoil him further."

This case has been described in detail because it illustrates the futility of believing that a single educational strategy can solve the interlocking network of problems generated by a learning disability. Jack's teacher, his mother, and his reading tutor all had different ideas about how Jack should be handled. They all had reasons for believing in their own methods—perhaps Jack behaved differently with each of them. Who is to help such a child cope with the problem of being caught in a web of conflicting therapeutic strategies? Until we find a strategy that works for sure, the answer is probably no one.

THE CASE OF PETER

Peter, who is almost twelve years old, is a much more serious case, as you can see from the two stories in (14) and (15). He represents a type of child frequently found in learning disability clinics—a child whose parents are above average in education and intelligence. For that reason, perhaps, Peter has been very well studied psychiatrically. There were reports from five different psychiatric consultations in his file, beginning at the age of five. These reports refer to difficulties—hyperactivity and speech problems—that had been present almost from birth.

Although Peter somehow managed to produce a WISC IQ in the normal range, his reading score, at the age of twelve, was at the early second-grade level. Essentially, Peter is a nonreader. His psychiatrist wrote four years ago, "Primarily his disturbance is in the reading-language area, etiology unknown. It is difficult to tell if it is neurological in origin, or psychological. It is probably a mixture of both, with the latter predominating. Whatever treatment approach is used with him, it will have to emphasize psychotherapeutic principles. The boy is emotionally unreachable right now and standard teaching methods will fail."

What the effect was of showing that report to Peter's teachers cannot be ascertained. At any rate, the teachers did see it, along with a covering letter from Peter's mother instructing them to "teach Peter psychotherapeutically" as recommended. Stimulant medication was also administered. (Peter has been on many forms of medication and diet.) By 1976, psychiatric reports were of this type:

> Peter performed as follows on the House-Tree-Person (drawing) test. The house is fantastically large, extremely primitive and literally covered with windows. There is no firm anchoring. He lacks a feeling of solid support but he certainly does desire interpersonal contact, although it is interesting that the windows are

His wallet was stolen from his locker. The coach will do nothing because he doesn't care. He is mad because the coach wouldn't do anything.

14. *Peter's Story 1.*

much more pronounced than the door. This suggests a somewhat infantile, exhibitionistic characteristic. He wants to be seen and noticed but he is not quite ready for genuine contact.

His figure drawing is a stick figure. He called it "the big boy—girl-boy—can do anything he wants." When he was asked to draw another figure he drew it extremely small, about half an inch and said "it's very small, too small to do anything."

The figure smiles. There are no ears. Again, we see a very regressed mental image of himself. He expects a lot to be done for him. It is still very hard for him to exert himself in any meaningful kind of way.

There was no question but that Peter was an emotionally disturbed child. He had been depressed, one would gather, practically all of his young life. "When asked if he ever gets sad," one of his doctors reported, "he said yes, every day. When asked if he ever got happy, he replied no." In the same report was the statement, "Motivation is weak. He takes the path of least resistance. He gives up easily and is impatient and impulsive . . . His

aney Palyer Cord of
solo The moeat. they
Cord of want into the
Loke room and tack moeat
from his Loke. becos someonn
was made at him,
becas he toke his pals on
the tame. end

*Any player could of stolen the money. They could of went into the
locker room and taken money from his locker. Because someone was
mad at him, because he took his place on the team.*

15. *Peter's Story 2.*

mood responses are almost solely at the depressed end of the
scale. He tends to be unresponsive to success and reacts strongly
to failure, threat of failure, or to criticism. He will often refuse to
engage in an activity because he is so sure he will fail." A portrait
of hopelessness. Peter was, then, seven years old and had already given up. Five years later he was somewhat more mature,
but he was still not learning to read.

Yet there is a ray of hope, almost a footnote buried in the
deluge of psychiatric descriptions and ruminations: as a boy,
Peter's father—now a lawyer—had also suffered from speech
and reading disabilities. Were his difficulties as severe as Peter's?

Is it in fact possible for a boy like Peter to grow up to be a successful professional man?

THE CASE OF SAMMY

Our last two cases are briefer and more cheerful. Sammy is a highly intelligent eight-year-old. As his story shows (16), he has worked out a phonetic system of writing which is serving him quite well, so well that one initially wonders if he had been taught another alphabet as a remedial device. (He had not.) According to his record, there were no difficulties until Sammy began school —except for one referral, at the age of five, to a speech clinic. Afterwards, he made good progress and did not require any further speech therapy.

His difficulties began when he entered first grade. He was reported to have started slowly and to have made little progress, so it was recommended that he be retained in first grade. He started at a reading clinic about that time, essentially as a nonreader. He began first grade again, but then his family moved and he was entered in second grade in his new town. Again, he had a great deal of trouble—limited attention, limited concentration, a lot of daydreaming, and now he is repeating second grade. Meantime, the parents were divorced. The father is college-educated, and both parents are very concerned about Sammy. The general family situation is intelligent and supportive.

Sammy's WISC score was unusual: his score on the verbal section was 115, and his performance score was 106—a discrepancy in a direction opposite to that usually displayed by learning-disabled children. But at the age of nine, Sammy's reading score was still on the first-grade level. Nevertheless, he gives the impression of being a child who will get things figured out eventually, and who will perhaps grow up to be someone who can write sensitively of what it meant to be dyslexic and of how the disability can be managed, even by children. Read his story again, and you will see what I mean.

THE CASE OF LUKE

Reading Luke's story (17) gives one a feeling that may be something like the feeling of a dyslexic child staring at normal print.

There wants was a man named fatso, thae call him fatso be cus he was fat. and he want to the dokr and the dokr sid he was gowing to die he sed to him self In got to ete alot befor I die, so easter came and he ascd for some hrd boyleags, and so thae brug him som hrd boyleags thae gav him 25 hrd boyleags, and he wet back to the doctor and he sed you our not gwing to die becquse you at hrdboiled* eggs.

There once was a man named Fatso. They call him Fatso because he was fat. And he went to the doctor. And the doctor said he was going to die. He said to himself, "I got to eat a lot before I die." So Easter came and he asked for some hard boiled eggs. And so they brung him some hard boiled eggs. They gave him 25 hard boiled eggs. And he went back to the doctor and he said, "You are not going to die because you ate hard boiled eggs."

*Teacher corrected

16. *Sammy's Story.*

A sakain.

A sakain is a Brid. I t have
a hand like a hrayl ando
bicd like a sru l ang buck.
To Back Feel. like read. ts and
The Fant Feet is like pics
and one wing is from a
Blue Brid and The clar
wing ic from a Brack Brid.
A Tall like A Dogand
ES like A cats it is
sAthina Tenin Fee T Tellehd
sATina Tenin FeeT Lame?

The sakarn stoye
He eats people and
Tars down honse and Fly
a arind spating Drad
Thit people

Then He Ppins /99/2

grins fa gus a day and, if
He bains /99,/12 grins
fo weaten a day.
It live in The martin[24]
and sarkes is /999,999 agd
and will live alar /999,999[130]
One day me and
my brith wit cut hunting
The sar kin Bit me cume not
Fied The sarking[153] use we
ontup in a Thoecater, bit we
come not fied me[165]

The translation of the first part of the story was not obtained. The last paragraph reads as follows:

One day me and my brother went out hunting the sark. But we could not find the sark. So we went up in a helicopter but we could not find him.

17. Luke's Story.

For instance, Luke intended the word Sakain to be pronounced "sark." He made up the story in response to an assignment to write a story 200 words long. He worked on this one for several months, and it is still not finished. The superscript numbers are in Luke's handwriting, and they refer to word counts—which appear to be accurate, if you know what the words are.

Luke is now almost thirteen years old, a cheerful, convivial soul. But there are hints of unseen depression. According to his mother, Luke is finding his inability to read at a level appropriate to his age and school placement extremely frustrating. She described him as being ashamed, frightened, and wanting desperately to learn.

But except for his reading problem, Luke seems singularly free of other difficulties. He had a normal infancy. He walked at the age of fifteen months, and began to talk well before the age of two. His file does show that he had a temperature of 106 at one point in his babyhood and had a convulsion. He also had pneumonia three times between the ages of three and four. There is a history of heart trouble in his family. His father—who is a clerk in a steel mill—has had three heart attacks at the age of fifty; and a nineteen-year-old brother has also had a heart attack.

Luke is the youngest of four children, all of whom seemed to get along well together. Luke has been babied, his mother says: there are many things he should do for himself, but which she or his father tend to do for him. At the age of thirteen, Luke is still somewhat afraid of the dark and does not like to go upstairs until a light has been turned on.

Luke's first school experience was in a church vacation school, which he seemed to enjoy. He then went to kindergarten, which was also enjoyable. In first grade, his difficulties began. The teacher thought he might have a vision problem, and this was found to be true (slight near-sightedness, easily corrected). Progress in learning to read remained extremely slow. Luke tended to confuse letters and to reverse words, as well as letters within words. Finally, in third grade, he was diagnosed by a school psychologist as having specific learning disabilities. He was assigned to a class for children with learning disabilities and remains in it to this day (fifth grade). He spends three hours a day in his special class, and then has art, gym, and music with the rest of the fifth grade. On the WISC, he has a verbal IQ of 98 and a performance IQ of 106, for a full-scale score of 102.

The impression one carries away from Luke's file is that he is a cheerful boy with a warm supportive family who is not overly concerned about his problem—except that it makes him unhappy. His father only completed eight grades and may also have had some learning problems, although nothing is said about them. But academic achievement is clearly not of great importance to Luke's family. One suspects that Luke's current depression and frustration—which is certainly not a chronic state with him—will disappear when he becomes old enough to leave a school environment that spotlights his deficiencies, and sends him on interminable hunts for a sark.

So, in our four cases, we have a child coping cheerfully with a learning disability (Luke); a child coping intelligently with a learning disability (Sammy); a child almost destroyed, emotionally, by a learning disability (Peter); and a child stressed by conflicting views of the best ways to help him (Jack).

There can be only one fundamental way of helping all such children, and that is to find out what is wrong with them. In Chapter 11 we will return to their stories and take a detailed look at their errors. In these error patterns there are clues to the nature of the scientific job that has to be done.

7 / Arithmetic Disability

The phenomenon called *dyscalculia* is broadly defined as an inability to perform the operations of arithmetic. As we will see, this is not a simple matter of forgetting a few numbers or rules. But we are far from knowing exactly what the problems are. Most of what we can say about arithmetic disorders comes from the study of brain-damaged adults, people who have suffered bullet wounds or tumors. It is not yet clear—as it seems to be in the case of dyslexia—that a similar type of brain dysfunction might be inborn in children who cannot learn arithmetic.

If there is such a thing as developmental dyscalculia, and if our knowledge of it must be shaped by our knowledge of traumatic adult dyscalculia, then what kinds of behavior should we be looking for? There are a number of guidelines in the pioneering work of the Russian neuropsychologist, A. R. Luria.

THE LOSS OF MATHEMATICAL SKILLS IN ADULTS

Luria's theory of brain function is compatible with the information-processing point of view to be described in Chapter 9. Essentially Luria believes that specific parts of the brain are responsible for specific parts of tasks. Imagery, for example, is thought to be a function of the occipital lobes in the back of the head. Any task that has an imagery component, then, would be disrupted by damage to the occipital areas. Luria's clinical descriptions are persuasive, but his theoretical views have not really been proven. The importance of Luria's work lies in the extent to which it makes us conscious of the many phenomena of arithmetic disability. Whereas we tend to think of a wrong sum as just plain wrong, Luria draws our attention to the subtle and complex forms that errors may take. Whether or not he is right about the locus of the brain disorders causing them, he is certainly right about the fact that the errors themselves are important scientific clues. Four types of arithmetic disorders have interested Luria.

Type I—Defects of logic.[1] Logical defects are revealed by a patient's inability to understand phrases like "a triangle below a cross" or "the brother's father." If such a phrase were dictated, the patient might write (or draw) the elements in the order they were named, without regard to relationships among the elements. Note that the relationships have a spatial aspect. To grasp them, one must hold the elements in mind simultaneously and compare them in some dimension.

Logical defects can also appear in the handling of numbers. For example, a patient might write the number 1029 as 129, thus demonstrating a failure to grasp the logic of zero as a placeholder. Similarly, the patient might write the number as 1000 29 —in the order the numbers were named, without regard to the relationships signified.

Logical defects of this type probably have their origin in spatial problems. Apparently what has been lost is the ability to maintain spatial reference points, such as the location of the tens, the ones, and so forth. "The analysis of compound numbers formed in accordance with the decimal system requires the differentiation of categories occupying different positions in space when written, and even when imagined they retain their spatial organization. It is clear, therefore, that when spatial syntheses are disturbed and . . . spatial ideas have disintegrated, the categorical structure of number is fundamentally upset."[2] Such patients also have difficulty understanding calendars and clocks.

The material in (18) was written by a twenty-four-year-old naval officer a few weeks before an operation for a brain cyst in the right frontal region, the same region Luria described as affecting spatial logic. We can see from the patient's writing that he also had difficulty orienting letters in words. He could not produce the digits 389 X 68 to dictation. When told that 8 X 9 = 72, he was not able to place the 72 properly. At the right of A is his attempted drawing of a man. The materials at B were pro-

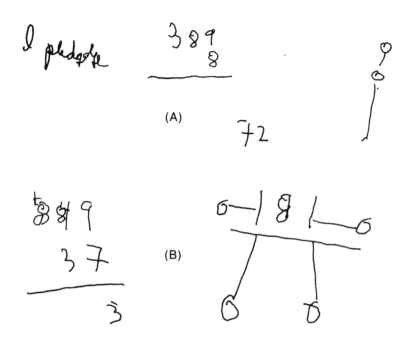

18. *Drawings of a brain-injured Naval officer. From Cohn (1971), in H. R. Mykelbust, ed.,* Progress in Learning Disabilities. *Copyright 1971, Grune & Stratton. Reprinted by permission.*

duced two days later. The ability to form the digits had deteriorated, and he could not complete the operations of multiplication. His ability to draw a figure was even more distorted.[3]

Type II—Defects in planning. Luria describes an adult patient who was given this kind of problem: "A boy is eight years old. His father is thirty years older, and his mother is ten years younger than the father. How old are they?"[4] The patient began to solve the problem in the following way: "Each part here must have thirty and then ten and then eight, that makes forty-eight and divide by three." The problem was repeated, and the patient realized that she had replied incorrectly: "I should have said the son was eight years old and the father thirty years older. I gave the wrong answer. I should have said the father was thirty eight years old and the mother, uh, the mother was twenty years old."

The problem was explained to her again, and she began to solve it correctly, although when she said "The father is thirty years older and the mother ten years younger," again she impulsively subtracted ten from thirty and concluded that the mother was twenty years old. Finally, the fourth time around, she got the problem right.

Luria said this patient and others like her regularly failed to perform a preliminary analysis of the conditions of the problem. As a result, the patient was never able to formulate a plan for solving the problem. Instead, the patient jumped into impulsive arithmetic operations and lost all connection with the original problem. Luria said she also regularly failed to verify her answers. Once she got some kind of answer, she was willing to settle for it. (Since this particular defect sounds very much like ordinary carelessness, it is most interesting to learn that it cleared up following the removal of a brain tumor.)

Type III—Perseveration of procedures that are no longer appropriate. Luria frequently tested patients on tasks of the following type: "On two shelves were 18 books, but not equally divided. On one shelf there were twice as many as on the other. How many books were there on each shelf?" The protocol of a patient attempting to solve that problem, along with Luria's comments on the protocol, are reproduced below.[5]

Protocol

The patient begins to solve the problem thus: 'On two shelves there were eighteen books . . . on one there were twice . . . no, that won't work . . . if they were equally divided there would have been nine.' But there were twice as many on one shelf. 'On one nine . . . no, then they would be equal . . . nine divided by two is four and one-half, that means four and one-half and twelve and one-half.'

Comments

The patient cannot reject the number nine, and in subsequent calculations he is guided by it, continuing to divide the number obtained by half. Solution of the problem is replaced by the formal rejection of a fractional part of the number.

'No . . . on one, four, and
on the second, fourteen.' . . .
Why four? 'Well, if it can't be
four and one-half, then it
must be four. The half is
impossible. Had it been 20, I
would have subtracted.

Luria then explained the principle of what he termed "sharing into parts" to the patient, who understood the principle and could apply it to new problems of the same form. However, when the form of the problem was changed, the patient crashed on the shoals of the new rule. New problem: "On two shelves there were 18 books, but there were 2 books fewer on one shelf than on the other. How many books were there on each shelf?"

Protocol

'That means, two books
fewer . . . perhaps nine and
seven.' How did you solve it?
'Eighteen shared by two is
nine, and then two fewer.' Is
that right? 'Sixteen . . .
No, there are eighteen in the
problem . . . These must also
be shared . . . by two . . .
they must be taken away . . .
Eighteen by two . . . there
were two fewer on one shelf
. . . we must divide into three
parts . . . On one shelf there
were twelve and on the others
six . . . Eighteen altogether.'
Is that right? 'No . . . there
were two fewer!' (Gives up.)

Comments

The old method of dividing
into halves springs out at
first, followed by the [new]
method of sharing into parts
[but] into the same number of
parts dictated by the previous
problem.

In the defects described thus far, the patients showed disabled organizational or procedural functions. They could calculate quite well. Precisely the opposite difficulty was shown by the next patient.

Type IV—Inability to perform simple calculations. This particular patient had been an artillery commander and had previously demonstrated a high degree of skill in performing gun-placement calculations. As a result of a bullet wound, the patient lost the ability to perform simple calculations of addition, division, and so forth, but maintained the ability to analyze problems and even to invent new strategies for circumventing his calculation defect. After his injury, the patient understood the logic of number and could still count forwards and backwards, even by twos or fives. However, he would have to go through the entire series, from the beginning, before he could produce the next number in the series. At first, the patient also appeared able to add normally, though slowly. But more careful analysis revealed that the patient was adding by counting. To add 17 and 20, for example, he would start with 17 and increment the number, by single units, until 20 units had been completed. The patient had no memories of addition facts or of multiplication facts —he multiplied by counting as well. "If they say: multiply 3 X 4, previously I would have replied immediately, but now I cannot do it, there are simply 3 and 4. I know that I should multiply, but all I can do is take it to pieces and add—3, and 3 again, and the same again a second time."[6]

The patient clearly understood the logic of multiplication, but the tables themselves had been wiped out of his memory. Nor was he able to relearn them very successfully. After a month of practice, he had learned the tables only up to five, and they had still not been automatized. When asked to multiply 3 X 2 he would work it out by counting. When Luria stopped the patient from counting by having him hold the tip of his tongue between his teeth, the patient became totally unable to calculate. "I can't do it at all, my tongue is held, and I cannot speak, everything is spinning round." The patient eventually became able to calculate with groups of five. "I can see that five is the same as five fingers, and these are all ready for use in calculation." He even developed a method of performing division by counting fives. "Twenty-eight divided by four . . . (thinks for a long time) makes seven. This is how I did it: I added the four groups of five, and got twenty, which left eight. Two will go into this four times; five and two make seven."[7] The patient was also helped by his memory of other highly familiar groups. For example, in the army he had called up his men three times a day, and a line of men was ten. Hence, the number eight could be recalled as "two missing from line of ten men." Although the patient gradually improved with practice, the old calculation fluency never returned.

What exactly was the nature of this defect? It was not simply a loss of number memory because the patient was able to retrieve any number by counting up to it. But counting seemed to be the only number-manipulation *scheme* available to him. By schemes, Luria meant highly automated calculation habits—into which numbers could fit. The patient did not lose the numbers; he lost the schemes to put them in.

In summary, then, Luria described a variety of arithmetic problems he associated with particular areas of brain functions. I have grouped them into four types: I, defects in number logic and in related spatial operations; II, defects in planning how to solve mathematical problems, including plans for checking the answer; III, perseveration of inappropriate procedures or ideas; and IV, inability to perform basic calculations.

FAILURE OF MATHEMATICAL SKILLS IN CHILDREN

It is instructive to compare Luria's cases with some described by Herbert Ginsburg in his analysis of children's difficulties in learning arithmetic. These are children who have no known form of brain damage.

Ginsburg is a psychologist who has specialized in the study of children's natural strategies for quantifying their world and for coping with formal mathematical instruction. His book, *Children's Arithmetic*, is a treasure chest of illustrations of children's spontaneous arithmetic thinking. One of Ginsburg's cases fits in with Type I above, logical defects that may have a spatial component.

Ralph, an eleven-year-old fifth grader working about two years below grade level, showed a . . . gap between written work and informal knowledge [of arithmetic]. Indeed, his informal skills were impressive. Given collections of objects to add (for example, 23 pennies and 18 pennies), he would group the objects and count by fives or tens. He solved mental problems by clever regrouping strategies. For example, to add 75 + 58, 'I took the 70 and 50, counted by tens and that made 120. Then I took the 5 from the 75 and that made 125. From the 8, I took 5 more for 130 and 3 more is 133.' He could add up to three digit numbers in his head in this manner. He was also adept at subtraction involving real objects and mental subtraction; in both cases he used grouping or regrouping strategies.

At the same time, Ralph's written computations were seriously in error. He lined up numbers from left to right, as in

$$
\begin{array}{r}
23 \\
+\ 5 \\
\hline
73
\end{array}
$$

He did not know how to carry. For example, given

$$
\begin{array}{r}
19 \\
+\ 16 \\
\hline
\end{array}
$$

he began to add from the left, doing $1 + 1 = 2$. Next he did $9 + 6 = 15$, which would have given

$$
\begin{array}{r}
19 \\
+\ 16 \\
\hline
215
\end{array}
$$

but somehow—it is not clear—he realized that 215 contained too many digits. His solution was simply to ignore the 5! this gave an answer of 21. In the case of subtraction, he was asked to do $15 - 7$ on paper (he had already obtained the correct answer in his head) and wrote

$$
\begin{array}{r}
15 \\
-\ 7 \\
\hline
65
\end{array}
$$

After having lined up the numbers incorrectly, he used the common method of subtracting the smaller number from the larger.

We see then that Ralph was skilled at arithmetic except when he had to do it on paper . . . Ralph would never work problems on paper, unless I told him to do so. And wildly contradictory answers didn't bother Ralph in the least. He seemed to believe that one gets different answers when problems are worked out on paper, rather than in an informal way [mentally], and that both procedures are correct. When I asked Ralph which answer is right, he said 'Both.' And when I asked why, he said 'It's different.' For Ralph, written work and informal procedures are separate, but equal.[8]

If Luria were to analyze Ralph's behavior, he would probably say that different parts of the brain were involved in the informal and written procedures; that the written procedures invoked spatial brain functions, while the informal procedures invoked motoric (physical grouping) and verbal functions (counting). Informal procedures can, of course, involve spatial processes, but with Ralph they probably did not. The case illustrates the very important fact that arithmetic logic, or the absence of it, can depend on the way the information is represented mentally—a fact repeatedly emphasized by Werner (Chapter 2). If Ralph were required to use a spatial representation, he appeared very illogical. If he were permitted to use an alternative representation, he appeared logical and clever.

But not all children are so efficient at switching from one representational strategy to another. Another of Ginsburg's cases illustrates Type III, perseveration of inappropriate procedures.

Patty was asked to write down the sum of 10 + 1. She wrote:

$$\begin{array}{r} 10 \\ +\ 1 \\ \hline 20 \end{array}$$

In an attempt to help Patty see what was wrong, the interviewer (I) said:

I: Well, suppose you couldn't use paper at all, and I said how much is 10 plus 1?
P: I'd count on my fingers.
I: Why don't you do it?
Patty held up all ten fingers and stared at them.
P: You have 10 (she looked at the fingers). You put the zero on the bottom (draws a zero with her finger).
I: Just use your fingers now.
P: Then you put 2 and you add 1 and 1 and it's 2.
Patty seemed unable to count 10 on her fingers! Instead she persisted in using the written procedure, apparently doing [it] in her head . . .
I: What about on your fingers? Show me how you do it on your fingers. You can use my fingers too. Put out your fingers too.
P: You put the zero on.
I: No, I don't see any zeros. All I see are these little fingers. Never mind zeros.

P: That's hard. (She looked as though thinking intently.)
I: Now you have all kinds of fingers to work with, Patty. Now you figure out how much is 10 plus 1.
P: You have to put a zero underneath.
I: I don't see any zero at all. All I see are these fingers.
P: O.k. If you want zero you have to take these ten away (she pointed to the interviewer's fingers). You put zero, then you have 1 and 1 left and you add them up and you get 20. So it's 20.
I: Can you do it without zeros?
P: No.

Finally Ginsburg made an important discovery about Patty. The use of the word *plus* was locking Patty into the inappropriate procedure. If the wording of the problem were changed to "How many are 10 and 1 *altogether?*" Patty would promptly answer "eleven."

> Given the word *plus*, she applied an incorrect addition method to both objects and written numbers. Given *altogether* she used a sensible counting procedure, again for both object and written numbers. *Altogether* is a natural word for addition. Patty probably used it in everyday life to talk about adding things. *Plus* is a school word that Patty seems to have associated with a wrong algorithm that she did not understand.[9]

Again, Luria would probably suggest that different parts of the brain are activated by the use of different verbal association networks. Changing a word may change a whole network of brain connections.

Still we must be careful not to overgeneralize from Luria's work. On the one hand, it is important to realize that arithmetic disability of the sort observed in schoolchildren can also be observed in adults who have suffered brain injuries. But we should not conclude that the disabled children have similarly injured brains. The most we can safely conclude is that some forms of arithmetic disability, like some forms of reading disability, may have a basis in brain dysfunctions.

A CASE OF DEVELOPMENTAL DYSCALCULIA

Arithmetic disability is seldom seen apart from reading disability. One exceptional case concerned a twelve-year-old boy who could read fluently but who had problems with spelling, as well as with arithmetic and with certain spatial tasks. The following description is taken from the case files of Norman Geschwind.

A 12-year-old boy was referred to the Aphasia Research Center of the Boston University School of Medicine because of threatened school failure. In particular, significant spelling disability jeopardized continued school promotion. He was the oldest child in a family of 4, the 3 younger siblings having no recognized learning difficulty. Both parents were well educated, and the father was a highly successful professional man. Birth and developmental history were entirely without abnormality . . . Spelling difficulty was first recognized in third grade and has persisted despite family and school efforts toward improvement. In striking contrast to the disturbance in spelling, reading ability has always been superior. In a test given in an excellent public school system, he was found to read 360 words per minute with 82% comprehension and thus ranked as the best reader in the school system for his age group. At the time of evaluation his reading activities were precocious. He had just finished reading *The Rise and Fall of The Third Reich* and was reading *Silas Marner*. He had read nearly all of the works of Poe, his favorite author. His hobby was stamp collecting but he enjoyed many participation sports including tennis, basketball, swimming, and football. Personal and social adjustments were excellent . . . A full neurologic evaluation revealed no abnormality . . . Spontaneous speech was fluent and well articulated . . . [But] in contrast to this ease of reading, there was notable difficulty in writing. His script was fairly legible, with small, clumsy letters . . . Sentences were simple in structure (almost always subject-verb-object) and the vocabulary was elementary, a striking contrast to his spoken vocabulary. When asked to spell specific words, the writing problem became more manifest. He spelled druggist as 'drugest', hospitable as 'hospitible', yacht as 'yought', and telephone as 'telaphone'.
    He could draw a circle, square, and triangle on command, but when he was asked to draw an animal, he merely drew a wavy line with a small circle at one end and called this a snake. He was unable to show the third dimension when asked to draw a box or a cube . . . A simple finger-localization test was given. With one hand behind his back and the other on the table in front of him, one of the fingers on the hidden hand was stimulated by the

examiner. The patient consistently failed to move the same finger of the exposed hand as requested [a demonstration of *finger agnosia*]. Calculations were done poorly and only at the simple rote-memory level. There was difficulty in column placement in both addition and multiplication problems. All calculations, even those in which he produced a correct answer, were done with effort, hesitancy, and uncertainty.

A full Wechsler Adult Intelligence Scale test was performed, showing a verbal score of 131 and a performance score of 101. The verbal score was uneven and depressed by a very low score in arithmetic, a pattern which suggests an even higher level of accomplishment in purely verbal activities. The family and the school authorities were informed of our findings and suggestions were made to both concerning management of his education. In particular, the school was encouraged to accept oral reports and oral test procedures. When last seen, the patient had not only attained appropriate promotion but was ranked in the upper one-third of his class.

Thus we have arithmetic disorders in adults who are brain-damaged similar to arithmetic disorders in children who are not —at least not as far as we can tell. A hundred years ago, a coincidence of the same type led Pringle Morgan to describe a syndrome we now call developmental dyslexia. Is there also a syndrome that should be called developmental dyscalculia? A special difficulty with numbers not due to poor teaching or to generally low IQ? I believe there is, and that it deserves more scientific attention than it has received.

8/Hyperactivity

Ever since the "Strauss syndrome," hyperactivity has been part of the general notion of learning disabilities. A current definition describes this malady as "A consistently high level of activity that is manifested in situations where it is clearly inappropriate, and is coupled with an inability to inhibit activity on command."[1]

In some cases, hyperactivity is simply an extreme form of general childhood exhuberance. In other cases, it is a reaction to environmental restrictions—such as being cooped up in a small apartment. In still other cases, it may be the reaction of a low-IQ child to a school situation that expects too much of him. In some percentage of cases, however, it is none of these. Instead, it is an inborn state of unknown cause, a congenital affliction beyond the control of either child or circumstance.

How do we decide if hyperactivity is present? One suggested set of criteria is listed in (19). As the list indicates, there is no single, clear-cut hyperactivity syndrome, and it is therefore difficult to estimate its actual incidence. In school, the syndrome may take the following form:

> His teacher may complain that he cannot stay in his seat, finish his work in a reasonable period of time, keep his mind on his work, stay at one task, refrain from calling out, and inhibit aggression . . . He makes many errors in both oral and written work because he does not stop to think. He seldom follows oral directions accurately . . . Once the teacher begins to doubt the child, her disbelief causes her to resent his interruptions and misbehavior, and this attitude is soon picked up by the other children in the class with the result that school becomes an intolerable experience . . . As his self-esteem continues its downward spiral, his per-

formance worsens and he is subjected to a barrage of deficit-amplifying feedback . . .
   Both the behavior and academic performance of the hyperactive child are very unpredictable, and this works to his disadvantage: A teacher who sees a child act like a disorganized tornado for the first two weeks of school and then suddenly switch to being obedient and industrious has a hard time believing that the child's behavior is out of his control. Furthermore, his grades often fluctuate from high to low, so that the teacher usually concludes that having done it once he could do it again if he wanted to . . . [However] the hyperactive child may *not* do better when he is trying his hardest and this idea is extremely hard for his teacher to understand and accept.[2]

Another symptom is the inability to inhibit *touching*. Ross and Ross consider this a sign of cognitive immaturity. Young children must manipulate objects in order to develop representations of them. Older children can represent them by names. Hyperactive children, Ross and Ross suggest, may lack more sophisticated symbolic representational systems. Therefore, they can know and understand their world—almost like blind children—only by manipulating it. Whether or not that hypothesis is true, it is certainly true that hyperactive children may grab, manipulate, poke, and push to an intolerable degree.

But if the child is *learning* from his touching experiences, then his IQ—especially during the preschool years—may actually be above average. I once watched a five-year-old boy, whom I would have diagnosed as hyperactive, in a laundromat. Among other things, he went all around the rather large establishment, repeatedly setting the door of each empty machine to the same degree of openness. That amounted to concerted practice in spatial estimation. Then he went from machine to machine (on top of them) pushing each coin lever in and out. That amounted to practice in gross and fine motor skills. And he had many other ways of occupying himself. The child had obviously learned more about laundromats than any normally active five-year-old would have. If he behaved that way continuously, then he was probably above average mentally—but would he hold still long enough to be tested?

The last question is a serious one and suggests the kinds of learning difficulties that eventually develop. As a child grows,

Overactivity (including unusual energy and restlessness) and Distractibility (including short attention span, never finishing work and projects) plus *any six* of the following:

Fidgets, rocks, etc.	Disobedient
Climbs on roof, etc.	Doesn't follow direction
Runs over furniture	Doesn't respond to discipline
Always into things	Defiant
Heedless of danger	Wakes early
Runs away	Hard to get to bed
Constant demands	Wets bed
Easily upset	Many accidents
Impatient	Lies often
Won't accept correction	Takes money, etc.
Tantrums	Neighborhood terror
Fights often	Sets fires
Teases	Reckless, daredevil
Destructive	Fears

19. *Criteria for the diagnosis of hyperactivity. From Stewart et al. (1970). Copyright 1970, Physicians Postgraduate Press. Reprinted by permission.*

he must adapt to a sedentary learning environment. Because the hyperactive child is—by definition—not able to adapt, he loses learning opportunities and falls behind. Eventually, the lag will be reflected in tests of achievement and IQ. It is for this reason that the hyperactive child may be classified as learning-disabled, even if no other difficulties (such as dyslexia) are present.

TREATMENT ISSUES

There is currently a great deal of controversy about appropriate treatment for hyperactivity. For a few years, it was thought that stimulant medication (often methylphenidate going by the trade name of Ritalin) would, paradoxically, reduce the child's distractibility and make him more reachable by instructional programs. Thus he would not waste the precious learning opportunities of childhood. Hyperactivity, it was thought, would be naturally outgrown during adolescence.

That last assumption has now been discarded. Follow-up studies have shown that hyperactive children grow up to be hyperactive adolescents and hyperactive adults. The nature of the hyperactivity may change, and in some cases it is probably more tolerable than others.[3] We all know adults who "can't sit still for a minute" but who yet keep themselves so usefully occupied that they would never be described as handicapped.

For a variety of reasons, it is difficult to do conclusive research on the drug issue. (Readers interested in the technicalities are urged to consult an article by Alan Sroufe.[4]) One problem, for example, concerns the use of placebos. To rule out the effects of expectation, children taking real drugs must be compared to children taking fake drugs—pills of the same size and shape that contain no medication. The problem is that the real drugs may produce side effects such as sleeplessness and occasional dizziness for a few weeks. Hence parents, teachers, and the children themselves can tell if the children are receiving real drugs or placebos. One experimental solution would be to put special drugs into the placebo pills—drugs that cause sleeplessness or dizziness and nothing else. Is that an ethical thing to do? Would you be willing to have your child participate in that type of experiment? Answers to such questions tend to be negative, so the conclusive experiment never gets done. What happens instead, as in the case of many new medical treatments, is that doctors prescribe drugs on a tentative basis and rely on reports from parents and teachers about their effectiveness. If the reports are positive, the treatment is maintained.

It is all very well to argue that the treatment may not be truly effective, and may even be doing more harm than good. When it comes to matters of human suffering, the right to try something that just may work is regarded, in America at least, as a fundamental human right. The suffering in this case is very real, a point made with great poignancy by children quoted in Ross and Ross.

> *Boy, 8 years, 6 months:* What I would like best of all would be to be like Jimmy Markhall. When *he* says the wrong answer the other kids all laugh but not like mean laughs and when *he* drops

something or knocks things down our teacher says, 'Oh, Jimmy,' but not being real cross and I would like that most of all.

Boy, 6 years, 11 months: . . . I would like it a lot if Mrs. Miller (teacher) would just once in a while, even once in the whole of second grade, say, 'Here's a boy who's really moving up fast' to me like she did to Stu and Jackie . . . And I also would like to do some things good like Elliot [older brother] does right from the start. Elliot hit a baseball right off, and he just catches good, and my dad says, 'That boy is a natural,' and I would like it if I was natural at something.

Boy, 8 years, 4 months: I just wish I could be just an *ordinary boy*, like I mean OK in school but not all A's and have the other kids ask me to play ball, and most of all I wish I could not cry when I get mad. It's really terrible when you can't stop crying and everyone's looking.

Boy, 6 years, 11 months: . . . I am very tired of everything always being wrong and having to go for tests and my mom and dad look awful worried and soon I might have to go to another school. And what I would like a lot would be if I could just sit still and be the way the other kids are and not have all these things happen. And most of all I wish I did not break that mirror at Teddy Work's birthday party.[5]

In consideration of their plight, it would seem only humane to put hyperactive children on medications which appear to help control and calm them. However, that decision must be made in light of the following facts:

—Medication for hyperactivity may suppress physical growth, at least temporarily.[6] Since mental growth has been shown to be correlated with physical growth,[7] it is possible that the medication may temporarily suppress mental growth as well.

—The ingestion of amphetamines may be linked to the development of Hodgkin's disease, a form of cancer involving the bone marrow. Since growth depressants obviously affect bone growth, there is the possibility of a connection between this factor and the preceding one.[8]

—The effects of medication on *simple* forms of learning—such as memorizing capital cities or the multiplication tables—is positive in some cases, but it may be *state-dependent*. That means the child must be in the same state during testing as during learning. If drugs were administered during learning, then they must be readministered during testing or the test performance will be worse than if no drugs were introduced at all.[9]

—The effect of medication on *complex* forms of learning—reading, writing, arithmetic problem solving, and other school subjects—has never been determined. We have no idea if drugs improve complex learning or not.[10]

—Alternative methods of managing hyperactive children with learning disabilities exist.[11]

MANAGEMENT OF ATTENTION

If we are ever going to resolve treatment issues, then we must examine hyperactive behavior in very fine detail. The Strauss syndrome described by the clinician, the "disorganized tornado" described by the teacher, and the sorrowful frustration described by the hyperactive child himself—all these are only gross pictures. Understanding the effects of drugs on behavior means understanding the effects of drugs on physiological processes involved in behavior. The drugs, after all, must influence behavior through physiological channels.

The sciences concerned with such matters—psychophysiology, and the like—do not yet have the answers we seek. They cannot tell us exactly how physiological reactions associated with methylphenidate get themselves translated into the behavior of lessened hyperactivity. But there are some theories about that, and current research is beginning to fill them in. I will describe one experiment in detail as an illustration. The theories generally concern the role of *attention* in hyperactive behavior, because attention problems seem to be common to all forms of the disorder. But exactly what is attention? Are there different kinds of attention? How can we measure them?

Porges' contribution. Stephen Porges and his colleagues at the University of Illinois have approached these questions in the following way.[12] First of all, they have proposed (as have other psychologists) that there are two kinds of attention: the kind you experience when something *catches* your attention; and the kind you experience when you deliberately *focus* on something. How might the two kinds of attention be measured? One common practice in laboratories of this type is to hunt for a physiological correlate of the internal reaction you are interested in. Porges and his colleagues used changes in heartrate as their index of changes in attention. Each type of attention, they hypothesized, should have a different type of heartrate change associated with it. When something catches attention, heartrate should quicken —almost the way it does when you are startled. But when you are deliberately focusing your attention, heartrate should slow down and become more regular.

To measure these two kinds of attention in school-age children, Porges constructed a simple racing-car game. First a "ready" light went on, and then a "go" light went on. At the "go" signal, the subject pressed a button that released a toy car on a track. The experimenter also had a car and a track and pressed a button too, but was not actually competing with the child (although the child thought he was). The child's task was to press his button faster than the experimenter pressed *his* as soon as the "go" signal appeared. If he did so, then his car would win.

The ingenious characteristic of this task was that it provided measures of both kinds of attention. The child could not predict when the "ready" light would go on—since the waiting period was variable. When it did go on, it caught the child's attention. Changes in the child's heartrate from a five-second period before the "ready" light to a five-second period after the "ready" light should therefore be an index of attention catching. We would expect the heartrate to increase during that period. The second kind of attention should appear when the child is waiting for the "go" signal. Presumably his attention is focused on the start button. Porges assumed this kind of attention would slow down the heartrate—compared to the pretrial rate—especially during his five seconds just before the "go" signal appeared.

So there were two kinds of measures for the two kinds of attention: the difference between the pretrial heartrate and the heartrate immediately after the "ready" signal was a measure of *caught* attention; the difference between the pretrial heartrate and the heartrate just before the "go" signal was a measure of *focused* attention.

Now, what about the effects of drugs? Ever since the Strauss syndrome, it has been assumed that there is nothing wrong with the hyperactive child's ability to have his attention caught. Too many things, in fact, catch such a child's attention. What seems to be deficient is the child's ability to focus his attention. If methylphenidate influences attention, then, we would expect it to influence only the second kind of attention, focused attention— that is, if it does in fact decrease hyperactive troubles.

Hyperactivity / 83

Porges' subjects were 16 children (15 male and 1 female) between the ages of 6.5 and 12. They had all been diagnosed as hyperactive and were participating in a drug-treatment program. Each child performed the car-racing task twice: once when receiving methylphenidate and once when receiving a placebo. Although, as noted above, children can sometimes tell when they are on a placebo instead of on a drug, it is unlikely that they would know how or when to alter their heartrate. So the experimental question could be reliably tested: would methylphenidate influence only heartrate associated with focused attention? The answer was yes, and (20) and (21) show some of the data.

(20) is a graph of the second-by-second heartrate just after the "ready" signal appeared. You can see that heartrate increased rapidly, as we would expect. You can also see that the same increase appeared in both the placebo and methylphenidate curves. The methylphenidate curve is generally a little lower (slower) than the placebo curve, but the shape of the two curves is the same. We would therefore conclude that the drug did not influence the children's ability to have their attention caught.

Now look at (21). This contrasts the pretrial heartrate with the rate just before the "go" signal, when the child's attention was presumably focused. You can see that the drug had a very marked effect. During the focusing period, the children on methylphenidate showed a reduced heartrate. But the same children on placebo showed an increased heartrate—just as they had to the "ready" signal. Porges believed that the faster physiological response was incompatible with focused attention—just as if a distraction were being experienced and attention were being caught by something irrelevant. (Recall the above quotation from Ross and Ross: "The hyperactive child may *not* do better when he is trying his hardest.") Therefore we would conclude that methylphenidate does help the hyperactive child to control and focus his attention.

IMPLICATIONS FOR TREATMENT

In the foregoing type of experimentation, only very simple tasks can be used. When it comes to complex tasks—like understanding an arithmetic problem—we do not know exactly when focused attention is operating. The mind works too fast, and we cannot open it up and see when it is focused on what. (Some of

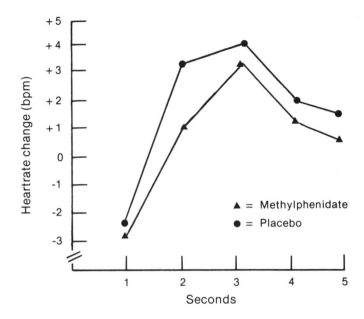

20. *Change in heartrate with onset of warning signal. From Porges et al. (1975). Copyright 1975, Society for Research in Child Development. Reprinted by permission.*

the newer techniques for examining complex task behavior will be discussed later.) That makes it difficult to decide if giving the drug is worth the risks described earlier. It would be safer to find some way of training hyperactive children to focus their attention—when and where they needed to. One method is described below.

Meichenbaum's contribution. Since Donald Meichenbaum, at the University of Waterloo, has recently summarized his own work, let him speak for himself. His main concern has been to teach hyperactive children self-instructional techniques.

> Self-instructional treatment can begin in the midst of ongoing play activities. The therapist can teach the hyperactive, impulsive child the concept of talking to himself . . . For example, while playing with one hyperactive child, the therapist said, 'I have to

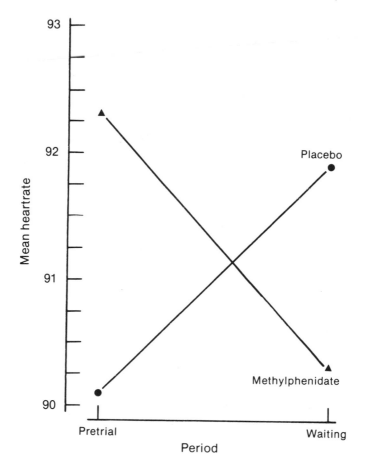

21. *Change in heartrate from pretrial level to level while waiting for the "go" signal. From Porges et al. (1975). Copyright 1975, Society for Research in Child Development. Reprinted by permission.*

land my airplane, now slowly, carefully, into the hanger.' The therapist then encouraged the child to have the control tower tell the pilot to go slowly, etc. In this way the therapist is able to have the child build up a repertoire of self-statements to be used on a variety of tasks. Training begins on a set of tasks (games) in which the child is somewhat proficient and for which he does *not* have a history of failures and frustrations. The therapist employs tasks that lend themselves to a self-instructional approach and have a high 'pull' for the use of cognitive strategies . . . Another technique designed to enhance self-control is to have an older, impulsive child teach a younger child how to do a task. The impulsive child, whose own behavior is actually the target of modification, is employed as a 'teaching assistant' to model self-instructions for the young child.

In using such self-instructional procedures, it is important to insure that the child does not say the self-statements in a relatively mechanical, rote, or automatic fashion without the accompanying meaning and inflection. What is needed instead is modeling and practice in synthesizing and internalizing the meaning of one's self-statements . . . The self-instructional approach to treat impulsivity focuses on the child's conscious self-regulatory ability. This also applies to the treatment of impulsive adolescents and adults. The child's behavior pattern is broken down into smaller manageable units and in this way the therapist tries to make the subject aware of the chain of events (i.e., environmental situations and behavioral and cognitive reactions) which set off the impulsive and often explosive behavior. This process is enhanced by performing a diagnostic evaluation of the conditions under which self-control is deficient. By making the child aware of the sequence of events, he can be helped to interrupt them early in the chain and to employ coping procedures.[13]

Meichenbaum's therapeutic strategies have an additional advantage: they help the child behave *intelligently*. Thus, practicing self-instruction not only helps the hyperactive child learn how to focus his own attention but helps him to overcome any associated learning disabilities as well.[14]

9 / The Information-Processing Approach

The concern of the information-processing psychologist begins with the fact that insufficient attention is being paid to what learning-disabled children are *doing*—as compared to how they are feeling, or how they are getting along with teachers and parents, or how they are managing their handicap. After all, the primary problem *is* the handicap. What is it? How can we help the child with that directly?

There is a great deal of basic research relevant to those questions. For the most part, this research is not known and utilized by practitioners in the field of learning disabilities. And the basic researchers themselves are only dimly aware that such things as learning disabilities exist. Hence there is a large gap between what is known and what is being done. I cannot, of course, close that gap here. But what I will try to do is sketch the nature of the basic research and indicate some of its possible applications.

THE COMPONENTS OF AN INFORMATION-PROCESSING SYSTEM

Cognitive psychology, or information-processing psychology, is devoted to the study of mental processes.[1] It begins with the notion that we have the capacity to make sense of our experiences. We pick up information and we organize it. Often we retain it and call upon stored information to assist us in managing new information. The fact that we make sense of our experiences, even though nothing ever happens to us in exactly the same way twice, must mean that *we* are organized. What kind of organized system could a person be?

We can use the diagram in (22) to help us think about that question. To begin with, a person has the capacity to pick up information of different kinds—visual, auditory, and tactual, at least. The pick-up systems are refined and sensitive. They do not detect a whole object or event at once. Instead, they detect very small aspects of it called *features*.

All of the features of an object or event are not picked up simultaneously. So there must be some way of holding on to the first ones while the later ones are being detected. We refer to these holding capacities as *buffers*—short-term memories for sensory information. There are probably several buffers, at least one each for visual, auditory, and tactual information. Information fades out of its buffered state very fast. If it is going to be integrated with other information, then the integration process must take place quickly, or there will not be any information left around to integrate. The integration of information being held in sensory buffers can be called *perceptual synthesis.*

To illustrate the first three processes—feature detecting, buffering, and perceptual synthesizing—consider what happens when you hear the word "cat." Your auditory feature-detecting apparatus picks up sound features, most of which are below your level of conscious awareness. A complex sound wave is nevertheless there and can be displayed on an oscilloscope. Features of the sound wave compose what we call consonants and vowels. The features picked up first—those involved in the "kuh . . ." sound—are held in a buffer while the rest of the sounds come in. All of the sounds are then synthesized, so that you hear, consciously, only the whole word "cat." This entire operation takes place at high speed, but it is possible experimentally to show that the stages described are actually there.

Similarly, with visual information, when you read the word *cat*—or even see a real live cat—you must pick up visual features, hold on to the early ones while the later ones are coming in, and put them together, at very high speed.

So far I have said nothing about *meaning*. We have a system that can organize featural information, but which has yet no way of representing what that information signifies. What does meaning itself mean, anyway? How do information-processing psychologists theorize about meaning?

Human semantic memory is generally considered to be an

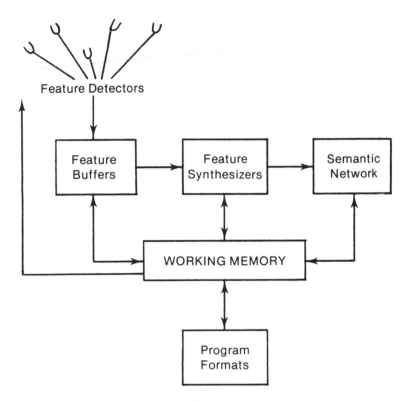

22. *A schematic flow chart of the human information-processing system.*

interconnected network of concepts—a *semantic network*. For example, suppose we were to list all of the ideas composing your notion of cat. The list would include ideas about fur, four-leggedness, tails, "meow," scratch, "Tabby," and so forth. Note that the list would also include information about how *cat* is spelled, how it is intoned, what the word looks like, and other symbolic properties—provided, of course, they have been learned. (My semantic list for cat, for example, does not include its Arabic spelling.) We call the property list a network because certain properties are connected to each other, as well as to cat. Fur, four-leggedness, and tail are interconnected—that is, fur reminds you of four-leggedness, tail reminds you of fur, and so forth. There are a great many experiments on such matters.

How do we conceptualize the process of getting into semantic memory? After the features of the word (or the object) have been picked up, buffered, and synthesized, the synthesized percept itself can be thought of as a *pointer* to a *switch* in semantic memory. That switch "lights up" all (or some) of the ideas you have about cats—the ideas listed above. The switch *is* the concept, and the switch is named CAT. Another switch, DOG or MOUSE, might light up some of the same parts of the network (those concerned with four-leggedness, for example), and we would thus say that one concept has "something in common" with another concept. In any event, if a synthesized percept switches on a collection of ideas—a concept—then we say that a meaning has been realized.

So far, we have been talking about a single perceptual-semantic operation—reading the word *cat* or recognizing a particular cat. But almost everything we do is much more complex than that. We read books about cats, draw pictures of cats, sew up pillows for cats, open cans of cat food, and so on. These are complex, organized, goal-directed *programs* that repeatedly activate feature detectors and semantic memory. While the program is being carried out, it resides in a *working memory*, where it is monitored. Many aspects of these programs are habitual or stylistic. An artist has a characteristic style of drawing cats, for example. These habits can be thought of as *formats*. We each have a storehouse of formats (rules-of-thumb, habitual strategies, individualized ways of doing things, and so on) that influence the programs we construct and how they are monitored. Most of the formats are adaptable in certain respects, but not in others. You can drive many different kinds of cars, but you would find it difficult to type on a reversed keyboard.

One informal way of describing a program is to write it out in a step-by-step fashion. Here, for example, is one way of showing what a program for copying a cat might include:

COPY-CAT PROGRAM

Step 1   Notice (first) set of features (perhaps the curve of the head and the left ear) and buffer them.

Step 2   Synthesize features into a unit.

Step 3   Transfer synthesized unit to working memory.

Step 4   Get drawing program from format storage.
Step 5   Set up objective (to draw first unit) in working mem-
         ory.
Step 6   Activate drawing program (begin to draw).
Step 7   Test: is the cat finished yet?
         If so, stop.
         If not, return to Step 1 (pick up the next set of fea-
         tures and continue).

That is a crude oversimplification of what actually happens. Each step of the program could be broken down, in turn, into a much finer sequence of mental processes. But even this gross listing makes it possible for us to formulate some useful hypotheses. For example, suppose a learning-disabled child is not able to perform this task very well. (*I* could not perform it very well, as a matter of fact.) What might be wrong? Does he fail to notice the right features on the cat he is supposed to copy? (I would not know *what* to notice.) Do they get muddled up, somehow, incompletely integrated? (The line from the left ear and the curve of the head would never get into my head as a unit; I might as well be looking at specks of pepper.) Does he have difficulty holding on to the percept, getting it into working memory? (I never get that far.) Does he have any drawing programs in storage? Does he know how to hold a pencil and make a line happen? (Just barely.) Does he have the idea of setting up the objective of drawing part of the cat, looking back at it, drawing the next part, and so forth? (No. I am programmed mostly for panic and flight when faced with a drawing task.)

The questions themselves quickly lead to more questions, and we soon realize that when we make such statements as "learning-disabled children have trouble drawing," we are not explaining what is wrong. To analyze what is wrong, we must find ways of monitoring the steps in the program. This is a difficult technological problem—because of the high rates of speed involved.

PROCESSING SPEEDS AND STAGES

Normally, an adult can register visual features (get them into the buffer) in about 50 milliseconds (msec)—that is 50 *thousandths* of a second. They will only last in the buffer about another 200 msec. If they are not dumped into the synthesizer by that time, they will have faded out of the buffer. Getting from the synthesizer into working memory may take another 50 msec, so that by 300 msec, at the outside, information has gone through the early stages of perceptual processing and has commenced operations involving working memory and semantic memory.

When cognitive psychologists design experiments, they usually have in mind some version of the theoretical system sketched in (22). Often they have worked out an explicit model (like the Copy Cat Model) of the particular experimental task being performed by the system. And their experiment is concerned with a specific step, or stage, of that model. They are asking: Is this stage of processing influenced by a particular variable (like an instruction, or a drug)? They can answer that question by examining the time course of the subject's performance. Does the variable influence one part (stage) of the performance rather than another?

Some scientists are more explicit about this than others. Porges, for example, did not include a diagram of an information-processing system, or a stage model of the racing-car task, in his published article. But his work is nevertheless relevant to that kind of theorizing. With a diagram like (22) in hand, we can say that the Porges experiment suggests that the early (perceptual) stage of *caught* attention was not influenced by the drug; but that the later (working memory) stage of *focused* attention was.

We might then ask: What is focused attention all about? What do you do, inside your head, when you maintain your attention on something? One thing you probably do is rehearse a self-instruction to keep your eye on something (which is one reason why Meichenbaum's therapy makes sense to cognitive psychologists). A follower of Porges might then do some new experiments to try to find out if methylphenidate facilitates *rehearsing* abilities or if it facilitates *talking to oneself.* Gradually, by such means, cognitive scientists are obtaining more and more detailed information about what is going on inside the head, about the stages and time courses of particular mental operations.

IMPLICATIONS FOR THE HISTORICAL MATERIAL

With this background, let us briefly review some of the older concepts already discussed.

Strauss' conceptions. Information-processing models—like the Copy-Cat Program—describe the hypothetical flow of attention from one mental activity to another. How might they help us understand attentional dysfunction? For one thing, tests like "Am I finished yet?" appear to be answered "no . . ." by a perseverating child. Or are the tests even made? Perhaps a defining characteristic of a hyperactive child is that normal self-testing procedures—checks and balances of one sort or another—are not made. They are not part of the child's model of a task. If Strauss' early guidelines are given modern empirical forms, new theoretical clues may become evident.

Werner's conceptions. The modern cognitive psychologist can view Werner's experiments and tasks as forerunners of information-processing theory. Werner was attempting to describe the *development* of programs for performing particular tasks—like an arithmetic task or the marble-board task. One of his hypotheses was that programs involving movements (counting on one's fingers, for example) were the foundation for programs involving images. This is an important conception, one shared by such theorists as Jean Piaget and Jerome Bruner, which has never been adequately tested.

Modern information processors would also be interested in finding new ways of examining Werner's discovery of particular performance strategies—as illustrated in (4). A child using a linear strategy, for example, would probably glance back at the model more often than a child using a constructive strategy. The "linear child" would not, presumably, maintain the whole pattern in mind, but would have to refresh his memory.

Hinshelwood's conceptions. Modern cognitive psychologists are very concerned with the problem of recognizing letters versus recognizing whole words. Hinshelwood's insistence that there are separate brain locations for these kinds of processing would probably not be taken seriously—but it has never been disproved. The fact that words can sometimes be recognized faster than letters has given rise to very intricate programs of research, which may or may not have moved us closer to a resolution of the issues. Massaro reviewed this material and concluded: "Given the current debate on basic issues in the identification of letters and words, it is evident that our current understanding may not be much greater than that available almost 100 years ago."[2] The issues are now defined in terms of stages of processing, steps in a letter-identification or word-identification program. Are features picked up letter by letter? Can features be picked up in parallel? Is the shape of a word a feature? Massaro believes, for example, that word perception is fast because of our knowledge of certain orthographic regularities—*q* is always followed by *u*, *th* is often followed by *e*, and so on. So a few orthographically regular features, picked up in parallel, would immediately trigger word recognition. It is not a different *place* in the brain that is being activated, but a different *program*—compared to the program for recognizing a single letter. But the thrust of Hinshelwood's theory has not yet been followed up: What is going wrong in the disabled reader?

Orton's conceptions. Orton was one of the first theorists to formulate the concept of *stages of processing* and to relate those stages to brain function. In modern terms, he was asserting that early perceptual stages were not dysfunctional in children afflicted with strephosymbolia, but that later stages were. This depends, we would now say, on the type of task being performed, and Orton would probably agree. Modern work relevant to Orton's main point—that something was wrong with left-hemispheric processing—will be given a whole chapter of its own (Chapter 12).[3]

IMPLICATIONS FOR MODERN RESEARCH

Information-processing concepts provide a useful framework for analyzing learning disabilities. To begin with, they make it possible for us to distinguish between the *system*—as diagrammed in (22)—and *programs* that utilize the system, such as the Copy-Cat Program. By definition, a learning-disabled child can process some information normally. If he could not, he would be called something other than learning-disabled. If his auditory feature-processing components never worked, he would be called deaf; if his visual components never worked, he would be called blind; if he could not hold anything in working memory, he would be called retarded or psychotic. In the learning-disabled child, certain information-processing components seem to go out of whack only sometimes, on certain tasks. For that reason, the problem seems to be primarily one of programming. Even if some subtle system defects do exist, there may be ways to program around them.

The important thing to remember about programs is that they are dynamic. They are streams of mental activities moving by at high speed. Something is held in mind, then something else is recalled, then some hypothesis is tested, then feedback is evaluated, and so forth, all taking place in a second or two. Information-processing research is guided by the supposition that one such activity (that is, one stage of a program) can be extracted from the stream and studied in isolation. (Several examples of how this can be done will be presented in the next chapter.) But this does not mean the activity will function equally well (or poorly) in any program that requires it. For example, recalling the names of your neighbors may be easy to do when you "go down the block" in your mind, but hard to do alphabetically. It would be misleading to diagnose you as a "good name recaller" or a "poor name recaller" without knowing what your mental program was. We might discover, however, that some children are poorer at alphabetic name recall than others are. If the former group had been diagnosed as learning-disabled by the usual school criteria, then we would have some interesting new information that might help us understand their disability. But we would not be justified in leaping to the conclusion that learning-disabled children can never remember the names of their neighbors. If we had used a spatial recall scheme instead of an alphabetic scheme, the learning-disabled children might even have outperformed the normal ones.

These are the main points to keep in mind, then, as you read the experiments in the next chapter: (a) a mental act is always part of a stream of activities, of a particular mental program; (b) the act can sometimes be studied in isolation, through special experimental techniques; but (c) any defects that are thereby discovered may appear only when the act is embedded in a particular mental program. The defect may disappear when the act is embedded in a different program. That is at once mysterious and hopeful.

10/Information Processing in Dyslexia

I have limited this chapter to studies of dyslexia because I know of no information-processing research on any other kind of learning disability—save the attentional research illustrated by the Porges study. There is very little work of this sort even on dyslexia. True information-processing research must permit us to make some inferences about the relationship of the research to a theory like the one diagrammed in (22) and it must involve at least an implicit model of stages of processing—that is, the experiment must provide some kind of data about what the subject is doing, inside his head, as he performs the task.

IMPAIRMENT IN FEATURE PROCESSING

The general problem at this level concerns the speed at which features may be picked up, buffered, and synthesized. Research on normal children indicates that these processes take place more slowly in younger children than in older ones.[1] Sensory memories (buffered information) are good in young children and last a relatively long time. In certain respects this is an advantage. It gives the children time to operate on the information, to adjust programs in working memory. But in other respects, a *perseverating* sensory trace could be a disadvantage, as we will see.

Dyslexic children, like younger children, may process perceptual information more slowly than normal children do—on certain tasks. An experiment demonstrating that was carried out by Gordon Stanley and Rodney Hall at the University of Melbourne.[2] They studied 33 children, about ten years old, who were 2.5 years below their proper reading level, but who were otherwise academically competent. Twenty-one of the children were male, as might be anticipated. Stanley and Hall tested the children in two ways. In the first test, the children were shown the designs in (23). As you can see, if the cross on the bottom left were displayed in the same location as the square, it would appear to be inside the square. Similarly, if the two right angles in the middle row were displayed in the same place, at the same time, they would compose a single cross.

Each child began by seeing a compound figure, like the cross inside the square. Then the figure was shown to him again, but this time the square was presented first, and the cross, 20 msec later. The child would still report that he saw the square inside the cross. Then another 20 msec was added to the delay interval, and so on, until the child reported that he saw two figures—first a square and then a cross.

For the normal children to perceive the two parts of the figure, they had to be separated by at least 100 msec. For the dyslexic children to perceive separation, the parts had to be separated by 140 msec. The image of the first part "stayed on" (in the head) longer than normal.

Recognizing that two different figures are there is not, of course, the same thing as knowing what they are. For the normal group to be able to say (or draw) exactly what the two parts of the figure were, the parts had to be separated by at least 180 msec. We can think of that as feature-synthesizing time. The first pattern needed 180 msec to get itself together before the second pattern was flashed on. The dyslexic children needed almost twice as much time to correctly identify the separated parts: 320 msec. If the second part flashed on any sooner than that, it interfered with the synthesis of the first part, and neither could be correctly identified.

In their other test, Stanley and Hall showed the children single letters, which were then covered up by a patterned mask (such as an asterisk). The children had to recognize the letter quickly, before their recognition process was stopped by the mask. The mask was delayed in 20-msec steps, until the letter could be recognized correctly. For the normal children, it had to be de-

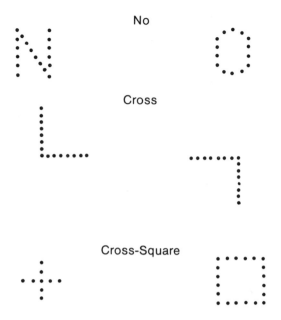

23. *Experimental stimuli. From Stanley and Hall (1973). Copyright 1973, Society for Research in Child Development. Reprinted by permission.*

layed about 50 msec. The learning-disabled children could not recognize the letter unless the mask was delayed for another 15 msec.

So not only was the feature buffer slower to clear itself out, but the feature synthesizer was slower to consolidate a percept— in the learning-disabled group.

PERCEPTUAL MASKING IN READING

Stanley and Hall were studying a task that is different from the task of reading. But it is possible that some of the processes they observed also operate during reading. To get an idea of what that could mean, look at the letters in (24). Look at the letter *o* in the top row. Notice how you can see the letters *t* and *s* quite clearly. Now look at the letter *o* in the second row. Notice how *t* and *s* are masked by the letters adjacent to them. Continue

t   o   s
nte   o   hsx

o
bom
sbomk
asbomku
easbomkut
geasbomkutc
wgeasbomkutcz
dwgeasbomkutczh
idwgeasbomkutczhv
xidwgeasbomkutczhvp
fxidwgeasbomkutczhvpn
rfxidwgeasbomkutczhvpnj
yrfxidwgeasbomkutczhvpnjl

24. *Letter display for studies of lateral masking.*

down the pyramid of letters, looking at the central *o*. Notice how the end letters continue to be recognizable, for quite a way down, even though the distance between them increases—but all the letters in between are a mush. When you set your mind (switch your attention) to pick up some of the letters in the middle, you can do so—but then the end letters wash out. In the process of shifting your eyes and your attention, these *lateral masking* effects come and go.

This masking is produced by three factors: (a) the similarity of contours (individual letters in the same type font are quite similar to one another); (b) the degree of spatial overlap of letters in the visual field; and (c) the amount of time that elapses between the visual pick-up of the first letter and the visual pick-up of the second one.

Normally, it will take a picked-up letter about 50 msec to register. If perception is interrupted by a second letter during the 50 msec, the first letter will not be seen. If a second letter comes into the system *after* 50 msec, there will be no interference. The first letter will have been registered, and the second letter will also be registered (provided, of course, nothing interferes with *it*). In that case, no masking will have occurred. If the two letters are far enough apart spatially, no masking will occur—no matter what the time parameters are. But where letters are close together, share similar contours, and enter the system erratically, then masking may occur. This amounts to a suppression or disappearance of certain letters.

When dyslexic children read aloud, they often say peculiar words. We usually assume that they are seeing the letters correctly, because they can tell us the letters, one by one, when we ask them to. But saying the letters, one by one, is a different task. During the task of *reading*, a child whose feature-processing system works slowly could conceivably experience masking. In (25) we see some words read aloud by dyslexic children. Were these children saying what they *saw*? If so, then what they saw was featural hash, very much like the hash that is produced by masking. Certain letters and even whole syllables were missing.

Dyslexic children may pick up letters from a line of print at a rate that is incompatible with their processing rates. Once the printed features move inside, they may move through buffers, synthesizers, or working memory, just slowly enough to be clobbered by the next incoming unit. If something of this sort were true, then it should lead us to design a whole different technological strategy for teaching dyslexic children to read. They should not be faced with a line of print, but with one letter (or perhaps one orthographic unit) at a time. These should be displayed on a scope sequentially, at a speed that is just right for the individual child. Or so the hypotheses might go.

Auditory processing.   So far, we have been talking only about visual features. But there has been evidence for years that

Test words (exposed for 2 sec)	What the reader said
bracket	"broket"
conceal	"concol"
kerosene	"konsen"
screw	"scree"
alternate	"alfoonite"
definite	"defynit"
estimate	"extermate"
majesty	"marijest"
solution	"slotion"
uncomfortable	"icomfort"

25. *Misreadings by dyslexic children. Data from Farnham-Diggory and Gregg (1975).*

something is wrong with auditory feature processing in some dyslexic children. In 1969, for example, Keith Conners and his colleagues showed that learning-disabled children had difficulty on a blending task of the type popular in phonics programs.[3] But an important recent line of research by Paula Tallal and her colleagues shows, again, how imperative it is to separate one stage of processing from another in order to pinpoint where a learning-disabled child's trouble may lie.[4] An ordinary phonics blending task is a very complicated program from the standpoint of information processing theory.

Tallal has been working mostly with aphasic children (who have difficulty forming speech but are of normal intelligence), and is only now turning her attention and technology to the study of reading-disabled children. By means of a speech synthesizer, she has experimentally manipulated speech sounds—so that an auditory discrimination task ordinarily failed by aphasic children becomes one they are able to do. The speech spectrum (the sound-wave pattern) produced by a simple sound like "ba" is very complex. Of particular importance is the high-speed wave *change* produced by the "b" sound. The change—the wave variation that you process in registering the "b"—takes place in about 50 msec (by now, a familiar number to you). But if—as a learning-disabled person—you cannot process featural information that fast, then you will mishear, or not be able to discriminate, the whole syllable. What Tallal has done is to get control of the speech wave artifically and to *slow down* the transitional speed of just that first part of the "b" sound. If she slows it down to 100 msec transition time, the children hear it correctly.

In her new work with reading-disabled children, she has found that *some* of these children show difficulties, similar to those of child aphasics, in auditory discrimination of speech sounds. Not all of them do, which has led Tallal to suggest, as have many others, that there may be more than one cause of disabled reading. If auditory processing proceeds normally, then something must obviously be wrong with other stages of the reading task. (A model of the reading task is provided in the next chapter.)

Tallal's research is moving us toward an understanding of the extremely subtle forms of functional deafness that may afflict some learning-disabled children. Some children may never have registered, learned, stored in semantic memory, those portions of the syllables that teachers want them to notice in phonics tasks. As a result, they may be unable to extract a phoneme from a stream of speech sounds.[5] When a teacher says "What is the first sound of *cat?*" they cannot answer because they have never really heard it. Of course they do not know that, and neither does anyone else, because no one has tested them on equipment that experimentally manipulates speech sounds. Some day, we may have hearing aids that do for speech perception what corrective lenses do for astigmatism.

IMPAIRMENT OF MEMORY PROCESSES

Unfortunately, we cannot stop the search for clues to dyslexic processing at the featural level. There is evidence that even when time is ample—when feature processing can proceed at its own rate, and successfully—troubles may still develop on particular tasks.

An experiment by F. J. Morrison and his colleagues at Dartmouth[6] would seem, at first glance, to contradict the work of Stanley and Hall. They used three kinds of materials: letters, geometric forms, and abstract forms, shown in (26). The forms were arranged in a circle, so that each form was equidistant from

| N | W | F | S | B | C | P | D | Letters |

| ~ | □ | △ | X | ⊛ | I | 8 | ○ | Geometric forms |

| ꙗ | ◊ | ◁ | 𝚔 | ↰ | ⟆ | ↶ | ⟋ | Abstract forms |

Complete set of letters, geometric forms, and abstract forms used in the stimulus arrays.

26. *Complete set of letters, geometric forms, and abstract forms used in the stimulus arrays. From Morrison et al. (1977). Copyright 1977, American Association for the Advancement of Science. Reprinted by permission.*

a fixation point in the center. The subject stared at the fixation point, and the experimenter then flashed on a stimulus array for 150 msec—long enough, as we know, for it to be registered. After a delay of either 0, 50, 100, 200, 300, 500, 800, 1000, 1500, or 2000 msec (unpredictably scrambled) an indicator appeared where one of the forms had been. The stimuli were changed around so that each position in the circle was used, and each pattern was used as a target for each of the ten delay intervals.

The subjects were twelve-year-old boys. There were 9 good readers and 9 poor readers (who read two or more years below grade level). The experimental question was this: "At what time delays will the disability appear? After 50 msec? 300? Or when?" Morrison's graph is presented in (27). It shows that no differences appeared between good and poor readers at early processing stages. If the indicator came on while the images were still buffered (within 300 msec), a poor reader, like a good reader, remembered exactly what had been there. He was not actually remembering it. He was, in effect, still *seeing* it in his mind's eye; it was still in his sensory buffers.

However, if the indicator was delayed by as much as 300 msec, the poor reader was in trouble. That may seem surprising in view of the Stanley and Hall experiment. One would expect the *perseverative* sensory images of dyslexic children to make them superior to normal children on the Morrison memory task. But this is just the kind of mistake that has led to confusions in

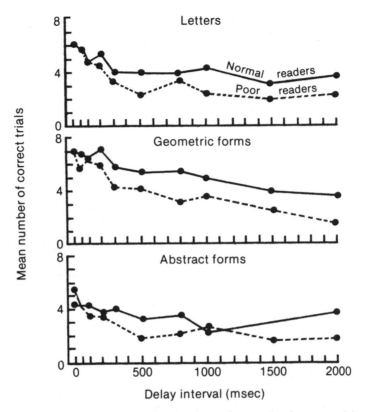

27. *Accuracy levels of normal and poor readers on the three sets of figures across all delay intervals. From Morrison et al. (1977). Copyright
1977, American Association for the Advancement of Science. Reprinted
by permission.*

the learning-disabilities literature. We have not been sufficiently
careful about task differences or about time differences.

In the Stanley and Hall study, perseveration was displayed by
dyslexics in the very earliest stages of processing, the first 50-300
msec. The Morrison experiment shows that the perseveration
does not continue indefinitely. Dyslexic children, like normal
children, must *act* on the contents of memory in order to pre-
serve it. The act of remembering is not a passive operation.

There must be programs for remembering, and they will involve attention, rehearsal, or other kinds of information management.

On another type of task, described below, there is evidence that dyslexic children do have difficulties with the kinds of strategies that might have led to success on the Morrison experiment —quickly naming a collection of things or scanning memory efficiently.

IMPAIRMENT OF THE ABILITY TO ACCESS SEMANTIC MEMORY AND TO USE FORMATS

Two experimenters at the University of California (Davis), Carl Spring and Carolyn Capps,[7] wondered, first of all, if dyslexics could name things—familiar pictures, colors, and digits— as fast as normal children could. That is a type of basic, very important question that we often forget to check out because it seems so trivial. It is far from trivial. A substantial component of almost any program in working memory will be names or verbal labels of some kind. A child may know those labels perfectly well. But if, for some reason, he cannot get them into working memory quickly enough, his performance will be impaired.[8]

Spring and Capps showed their subjects (in the seven- to thirteen-year age range) 25 pictures of common objects (wagon, duck, leaf, cat, etc.), 30 color patches of familiar colors (red, yellow, blue, etc., repeated unsystematically), and 50 randomly sequenced digits (one-syllable digits only, which meant that 0 and 7 were excluded, as well as all the numbers after 10). Digit naming was tested twice. The children were instructed to name the items as fast as they could, and naming speeds—in terms of the number of items named per second—were then computed. (28) shows what they were for children of different ages and different reading capabilities. (The young children were between 7.5 and 10.0; the middle age group ranged from 10.0 to 12.0; and the oldest group, from 12.5 to 13.5.)

As we can see, naming efficiency increased with age. We can also see that the normal readers (solid lines) were generally faster than the poor readers, especially on naming digits. So we should keep in mind the possibility that dyslexic children may have difficulty with some tasks that depend on naming speeds. How-

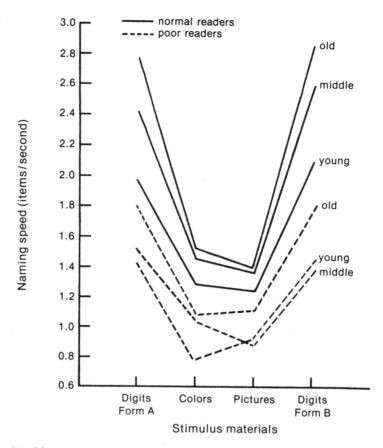

28. *Mean naming speeds of dyslexic and normal boys for digits, colors, and pictures. From Spring and Capps (1975). Copyright 1975, American Psychological Association. Reprinted by permission.*

ever, that does not mean they will have difficulty with all such tasks. The degree of impairment would depend upon the way naming skill entered into a working-memory program. Spring and Capps thought, for example, that naming speed might influence rehearsal in tasks that had a fixed time limit. If it takes you a long time to name something, then you will not have much time left to go over it.

They examined rehearsal skills by having the children play a form of Concentration. Eight cards containing the digits 1 through 8 were shown to each child, one at a time, at a one-second rate, and were then placed face down in a row (from the subject's left). A new card with one of the digits on it (the probe digit) was then shown. The child's job was to point to the card that he thought contained the matching digit.

Not surprisingly, the last one or two cards presented are generally the easiest to remember—psychologists call this the *recency effect*. So are the first one or two cards—this is called the *primacy effect*. The primacy effect appears because we have had more time to rehearse the very first cards that were presented than we have had to rehearse the cards in the middle of the series. So there are different reasons for primacy and recency: primacy results from rehearsal, but recency results from the fact that the sensory images are still fresh.

What kind of evidence might there be that rehearsal is in fact taking place? Spring and Capps decided to record the subjects' eye movements. They reasoned that subjects who were scanning the cards from left to right, which was the order of their appearance, were probably rehearsing the cards in that order. If so, then those subjects should display a strong primacy effect: (29) shows they did. In the first place, all but one of the good readers were scanners, but only half the poor readers were scanners. The nonscanners were not very often correct on the first two or three cards; they were not showing a primacy effect. The scanners, whether good readers or poor readers, showed a much stronger primacy effect. The overall performance of the poor readers was, however, worse than the performance of the good readers —except on the very last trials. This suggests that nothing was wrong with the buffered (recency) memories of the poor readers on this visual task. But there was quite a bit wrong with the rehearsal (primacy) capacities of some of them.[9]

Spring and Capps believe the deficiencies resulted primarily from the fact that the poor readers were slow to name items— not just digits, but slow to name anything. Because of this naming lag, the poor readers had little time for rehearsal. In fact, whether rehearsal would even be *attempted* or not (that is, whether the scanning format would even appear in the subject's behavior) could be predicted from his naming speed. Subjects who could not name simple objects at a rate of at least one per second did not even try to use a scanning strategy during the concentration task.

IMPAIRMENT OF THE ABILITY TO COORDINATE INFORMATION OVER TRIALS

One final experiment illustrates still another factor—how the processing capabilities of dyslexic children may change with repeated trials. Whether we call these *practice* effects or *fatigue* effects will depend upon whether the performance gets better or worse. In either event, it is important to look at trial effects in experiments like those I have been describing.

A task that measures short-term memory, auditory or visual, is just another task being conducted in working memory. It should not be concluded from impaired performance on that task that a child has a general working memory impairment. If he did, then he would be quite unable to function in the everyday world. But a child may have trouble managing information of one particular type—holding letter sounds in mind, say, while performing particular operations on them. Since that kind of task often appears during reading instruction, we have good reason to worry about children who are unable to do it.

Lee Gregg, a colleague at Carnegie-Mellon University, and I examined the short-term memory functioning of fifth-grade normal and dyslexic children on two kinds of tasks.[10] In the first task, called *memory span*, letters were presented to the children, one by one, in either the visual or the auditory modality. In the visual modality, the letters were presented serially, just as they were in the auditory modality. After four letters had been presented, the child said them back. He did this ten times in each modality.

In the second task, called *memory scanning,* we tried to get at some of the ways in which children, learning to read, have to use their memories. One common school task, for example, is recalling what letter a word begins with. Or sometimes a child must scan a word, in his memory, and decide what letters (or sounds) came in the middle. So our memory-scanning task presented four letters, in sequence, and then asked such questions as: "Which letter came first?" There were 40 trials. Both visual and

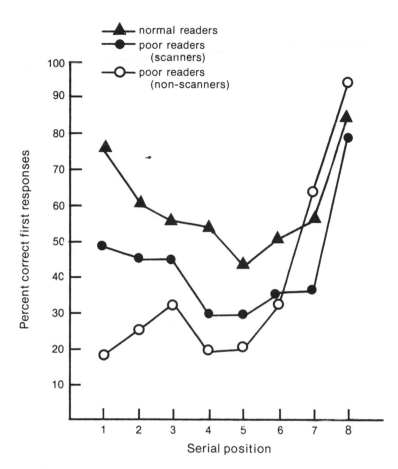

29. Percentages of correct first-choice responses at each serial position for dyslexic boys (scanners and nonscanners) and normal boys. From Spring and Capps (1975). Copyright 1975, American Psychological Association. Reprinted by permission.

auditory materials were used, and we measured the speed of the child's correct answers—how fast he could operate on the letters in his working memory.

We were, of course, interested in accuracy, but we were even more concerned with the children's *performance over time*, during an entire set of trials. Here was where we found major differences between the dyslexic and normal children.

Look at (30), which shows what happened on the memory-span trials within each modality and also what happened when the modalities were switched. At the left of (30) we can see that the good readers started the visual task at a level of about 80 percent correct. At the end of their 10 trials, they dropped to 65 percent correct. That is a perfectly normal phenomenon. It can be thought of as memory fatigue arising from repeatedly doing *exactly* the same thing. If there is even a slight change in what you are doing, the fatigue effects may disappear. After the normal children completed the visual memory-span trials, they were given the auditory series. You can see that their first two trials on the auditory materials bounced back up to 90 percent correct. Their memory fatigue disappeared because they had switched to another modality.

The same effects appear on the right side of (30) for the normal children. This time, the auditory task was presented first. The children were 80 percent correct at the beginning, and 68 percent correct at the end. When the visual task was then introduced, the normal children bounced back up to 90 percent accuracy.

Now look at what happened to the poor readers. When they began with the visual task, they produced the highest scores of anyone—a flat 100 percent correct over the first two trials. By the end of the visual trials, they had dropped down to 50 percent correct. When they then started the auditory trials, however, there was only a very slight recovery effect. The poor readers started the auditory memory span task at 68 percent correct, about where the normal children ended up. For the dyslexic children, switching modality brought little release from memory fatigue.

The situation is even worse in the right half of the figure, where the auditory task was presented first. The poor readers started out at a normal level (80 percent correct), and ended the auditory trials at 68 percent correct. But then, when the visual trials began, no recovery whatsoever was displayed. Those trials began at only 50 percent correct and ended at a 40 percent level.

We can see from this why there are arguments among researchers about whether poor readers have good or poor auditory or visual short-term memory capacities. The answer you get may depend upon what stage of a memory span task you

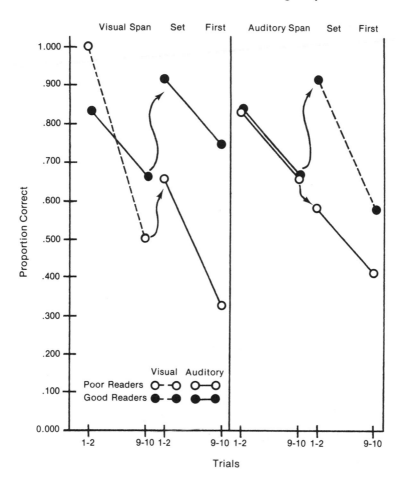

30. *Proportion of first two and last two trials correct, on auditory and visual memory span trials. From Farnham-Diggory and Gregg (1975). Copyright 1975, Academic Press. Reprinted by permission.*

sample. If we looked only at the first one or two trials of the visual span task we would decide that the dyslexic children were *superior* to normal children. Note, however, that there never seems to be any occasion when the dyslexic children show auditory memory skills that are superior to those of normal children.

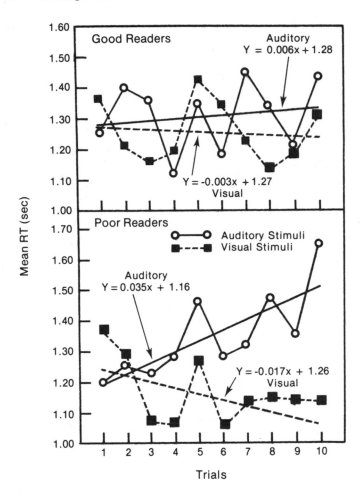

31. *Synchrony and asynchrony in memory scanning RT of good and poor readers. From Farnham-Diggory and Gregg (1975). Copyright 1975, Academic Press. Reprinted by permission.*

When we examined memory scanning, another aspect of the visual-auditory coordination problem became apparent. This is shown in (31). You can see that the visual and auditory memory-scanning speeds changed over time. In the group of good readers, this change was not very great. That means the speed at which a good reader could scan visual memory sets remained about the same as the speed at which he could scan auditory memory sets. But for the poor readers, the situation was different. As time went on over trials, their ability to scan auditory elements in working memory became fatigued, while their ability to scan visual elements became more and more efficient. Thus a large discrepancy developed between auditory and visual memory-scanning speeds.

Consider what this implies. As we point out in our original report, "Auditory-visual scanning synchrony may be critical to the efficient flow of the reading process. If, as seems to be the case for poor readers, auditory retrieval gradually lags relative to visual retrieval, a devastating type of asynchrony could result: Attention to a visual particle would move on before the auditory associate could be retrieved."

We have analyzed several experiments in detail as a way of illustrating how information-processing psychologists investigate the problem of dyslexia. They are all working within the framework of a model similar to the one sketched in (22), although they may favor other variations of it. Gradually, the picture will fill in. Little by little, fact by fact, science will be able to formulate an integrated theory of dyslexia. In the meantime, there is no way we can put the results of a few early experiments together and produce such a theory. The most we can say is that there is some preliminary experimental evidence that dyslexic children, compared to normal children, have problems with particular stages of particular task programs. Of equal importance is the fact that they do not have problems with all stages, and that they can *do* the tasks. It is as if we were beginning to look at mental processes through a very low-powered, blurry microscope. We can tell that there are some performance differences between normal and dyslexic children, and we can tell that we are on the right track by doing a type of research that permits us to dissect a performance into parts (stages) and to examine each part separately. But we cannot see more clearly at the present time. Clarification will depend upon the invention of new and better psychological microscopes.

11/Reading and Spelling Protocols

In the foregoing research, *groups* of children have been studied. Researchers have been looking for signs that—despite the differences among children—some aspect of their behavior will be essentially the same. A pattern of response from one child, though difficult to extract from the complexity of his surrounding activities, may resemble the pattern of response from another child. As the children are added together, the pattern is intensified and we become able to see it more clearly.

Patterns are all-important in the development of theory. But when it comes to handling an individual child, we may be less interested in what he has in common with other children than in how he differs from them. The research just reviewed suggests that there are many ways in which information-processing programs could be defective. Thus we must at some point assess the unique programs of the particular child. One technique of information-processing psychology, *protocol analysis,* is especially useful for that purpose.

Protocol analysis differs from task analysis in several ways. Protocol analysis is based on behavior—on a sample of what the individual has actually been doing in the course of solving a problem, or writing a word, or "thinking out loud." Task analysis is a theory or model of what he might have done—of what the task is all about. The Copy-Cat Program is one example. A protocol analysis helps you to construct the task model. The model, in turn, helps you interpret new protocols. Without a model, you may not recognize what is important about a protocol. A model of a task is essentially a set of guidelines for understanding how people do the task. A protocol is a "print-out" of what was actually done.

The application of protocol analysis to learning disabilities amounts to a new diagnostic system, as we will see. It is informal and, like all informal methods, relies upon the sensitivity and intelligence of the diagnostician. But it does keep one focused on what the child is actually doing rather than on extraneous interpretive matters. And, most important, it generates remedial ideas. As soon as you begin to pay close attention to the fine detail of a child's behavior, you find yourself saying, "Aha, *that* might be the problem, and *this* teaching strategy might help."

In this chapter, we will look at two samples of learning-disabled behavior: the behavior of a dyslexic girl trying to sound out a word; and some of the spelling errors of the four children in Chapter 6.

A READING TASK

I begin with an informal analysis of a very common reading task—sounding out a word. What must a child do, inside his head, in order to sound out a word? We suppose that the following steps are involved:

SOUNDING-OUT PROGRAM

Step 1	Select a set of letters.
Step 2	Find their sounds in semantic memory.
Step 3	Articulate the sounds.
Step 4	Hold the sounds in working memory.
Step 5	Test: is the word finished yet? If not, return to Step 1 (select the next letter set). If so, go to Step 6.
Step 6	Integrate the sounds being held in working memory (blend).
Step 7	Test: do I recognize the word? If not, return to Step 6 (try another integration). If so, stop.

Now we must obtain some protocol data.

The world is, of course, full of data. Our problem is to get data in a form that can be matched to the steps in our program.

Suppose we give a child a sounding-out word test, either an informal one or a standardized one. At the end of that test, we would have a single number, a test score. That score could be compared to other children's scores or even to a population of scores. But does this tell us anything about how the child's mind worked *during the production of that score?* The answer is no. Specifically, there is no way we can match up that number to the steps in our informal program.

To perform a processing analysis, we must get process data— a record, in real time, of what the individual is doing. In the case of a sounding-out task, we could tape-record the child during the sounding-out process. (32) is the protocol of a fifth-grade dys-

Line number	Spoken particle
1	s
2	so
3	ll
4	ut
5	tay
6	ny
7	so
8	tu
9	nay
10	ny
11	so
12	lliu
13	so u
14	tay
15	ny
16	so
17	so lu tay ny
18	"I think that's right"

Total sounding-out time: 44.8 seconds.

32. *Sounding-out protocol of a ten-year-old dyslexic girl reading the word "solution."*

lexic girl, called Jenny, sounding out the word *solution*. We just wrote down, in order, whatever Jenny said. Whenever she paused, we put the next syllable on a next line, and numbered the lines for convenience.

Now we can compare our sounding-out process protocol to our sounding-out process program.

Lines 1 and 2 (Steps 1-3 of the model; also Steps 4, 5?)	Jenny appears to have picked up the initial letters, found their sounds, and articulated them correctly. So far, so good.
Lines 3 and 4 (Steps 1-3; also 4, 5?)	Possible problem: Jenny is picking up the l by itself, and the *ut* as a separate particle. One suspects that a skilled reader does not visually parse the word in that way. The skilled parsing is probably *so-lu-tion*. Instead, our child has visually parsed the word into *so-l-ut* . . . so we foresee trouble.
Lines 5 and 6 (Steps 1-3; also 4, 5?)	Here comes the trouble: *tion* is being sounded-out as "tay" and "ny." That seems remarkable, in view of the fact that *tion* is an extremely common pattern and is taught specifically in phonetics lessions. Where did the "tay" come from? Is *i* being seen as *a* in Step 1 of the process? Or is *i* being seen correctly but is calling up the wrong sound—in Step 2 of the program? And what about the "ny"? That probably should have been transcribed *ni;* it probably is the *n* and the *i*—in the wrong order —from *tion*. In that case, the

"tay" may be a combination
of the *t* and the *o* (which is
either seen as *a* or is being
given an "ay" sound). So we
have *tion* turned into "tay"
(for *t__o__*) and "ni" (for
__*i*__*n*).

Up to this point, we cannot be sure Jenny is actually proceeding through Steps 4 and 5 of the program—holding the sounds in working memory (Step 4) and performing the test in Step 5 (finished yet?), the answer to which is no, which then sends the child back to Step 1 again to pick up the next set of letters. But now we can see that these steps were apparently occurring. Otherwise the next steps would not have been possible. That is the good news. The bad news is that Jenny is remembering what she *said* ("nay" and "ni"), even though what she said was wrong. Once the integration phase of the sounding-out process begins (Steps 6 and 7), it operates on the *sounds* being held in working memory, regardless of what they are.

Lines 7-10
(Steps 6 and 7)

The child's stated "so-tu-nay-ni" reveals that the sound particles *were* being held in working memory and were integrated (Step 6). However, when the test at Step 7 is performed, the child apparently decides that she has not integrated the particles correctly (the problem was the second particle "tu") and so she tries it again.

Lines 11-12
(Steps 6 and 7)

Here, she corrects the "tu," and interestingly shows that a portion of the particle stream could be corrected without dislodging the rest of the stream—which is apparently still available to working memory for integration.

Lines 13-15 (Steps 6 and 7)	Again, the integration is tried, tested, but still does not pass the test.
Line 16 (Step 6)	The integration is attempted again.
Line 17 (Steps 6 and 7)	And again—this time so quickly that we would not feel justified in placing the particles on separate lines: the pauses between them are too short.
Line 18	"I think that's right" shows us that Jenny now believes she has recognized the word, that the test at Step 7 has been passed affirmatively.

The example has shown not only how the child's mind may have worked, but also how the mind of the diagnostician has worked—how one sets up a model, collects data in a form that can be compared to the model, and then goes about the job of matching and interpreting. We can continue in this mode by asking: What research should we look toward for help in understanding the phenomena?

Lines 3-6 of the protocol raise the first important question: Why is Jenny visually parsing the word in this manner? It would be useful to know a great deal more than we do about how children naturally parse words, what they think are the natural divisions for sounding out places of words. Our particular subject was a ten-year-old girl of normal intelligence who had been receiving remedial reading instruction for some time. (In fact, according to her reading teacher, Jenny was supposed to know the word *solution*.) It was probably not the case that the girl's idiosyncratic parsing (so-l-ut . . .) reflected merely a developmentally younger view of how the word should be parsed. But it would be helpful to be sure of that, to have tables showing how children of different ages, and probably with differing amounts of phonetic instruction, decompose words into units they think should be pronounced.

A related question concerns Jenny's own theory of the sounding-out process. Perhaps she views it as a one-letter-at-a-time procedure. Again, I know of no research on that specific question; it is assumed that the teacher's rules have been more or less adopted by their pupils. But Jenny may have invented a different set of rules, ones that were not working especially well but that she at least felt she understood.

These first two questions—how does the child think words are parsed? and how does she think the sounding-out process is supposed to work?—concern Jenny's store of formats, strategies she has constructed and stored for dealing with information. But information may have rules of its own. Has Jenny noticed and stored orthographic regularities of the written language—such as *tion?* Why was that not recognized? There are a number of possible reasons: (1) the pattern might not have been correctly perceived at the time of sounding out; (2) the pattern might not have been correctly perceived at an earlier period in Jenny's development, when orthographic regularities were being initially learned; (3) the regularities might not have been remembered, a storehouse of familiar patterns might not have accumulated in Jenny's semantic memory; or (4) the sound "shun" might not be strongly enough associated with *tion,* although Jenny, who can talk quite normally, uses "shun" fluently in her spoken language. A strong sound association ("shun") might have prevented *tion* from fragmenting into *ta* and *ni.*

These are provocative speculations. There does exist research on some of them, and we have ways of gathering relevant data on groups of normal or learning-disabled children. But such general information will not tell us what is wrong with any particular child. There is urgent need for diagnostic procedures that can be used to probe a given child's particular problems with particular school tasks. We should be able to find out about Jenny, as soon as she manifests a reading difficulty:

What is her parsing system?
What are her personal rules for performing the task?
Does she see stable letter patterns?
Does she have a stock of stable letter patterns in memory?
Does she know what those patterns sound like?

We could add dozens of questions to that list. Even a crude attempt to find answers for a particular child can open up a whole new world of remedial possibilities.

A SPELLING TASK

Let us now look at the task of writing a word. What is it we do? Informally we can construct the following model:

WRITE-A-WORD PROGRAM

Step 1	Choose a word that means what you want it to, in context.
Step 2	Hold its overall sound in working memory.
Step 3	Select a sound particle (probably the first syllable).
Step 4	Find an associated letter pattern in semantic memory.
Step 5	Write the letters down.
Step 6	Test: do I recognize the pattern I wrote? (Does it "look right"?) If not, return to Step 4. If so, go on to Step 7.
Step 7	Test: is the word finished yet? If not, return to Step 2 (continue). If so, stop.

When a sounding-out and a writing program are compared, it is clear why writing is so much harder. There are more activities, more tests, and more ways of becoming confused.

For data, we can examine the words written by the four children seen in Chapter 6. Some of their misspellings are shown in (33). One important question is this: Do the individual children appear to break down at different stages of their modeled processing?

Take Jack, for example. Certainly he is choosing his words meaningfully. He has specific objects or events in mind, and he knows what words represent them. So Step 1 of the model is executed successfully. What about Step 2? Is Jack holding the overall sound patterns in mind? He seems to have the right number of syllables and essentially the right inflection represented in *poises*, *vitem*, and *morer*. But what about *enpery*? That contains one more syllable than *empty* does. Did he mean to write the equiva-

Jack	Sammy	Peter	Luke
poises (poison)	thae (they)	chcah (coach)	brith (brother)
vitem (venom)	dokr (doctor)	croc (care)	sakain (sark)
enpery (empty)	boyleags (boiled eggs)	anethank (anything)	grins (gallons)
lenan (lawn)	gowing (going)	moeat (money)	wit (went)
morer (mower)			throccatei (helicopter)
enperd (emptied)			

33. *Some misspellings of the four children during creative writing.*

lent of *enpry*? *Enperd* is a plausible past tense spelling of *enpery*, so we should not be too quick to discount the second *e*. *Lenan* (lawn) also may have an extra syllable. Is that an enlarged sound pattern? Overall, I would not be confident that Jack is capable of getting through Step 2 without difficulties. But if he is getting through it, then surely he is having trouble with Step 3—distinguishing phonemic particles. Once past Step 3, however, the rest of the task seems to be managed efficiently. Jack finds plausible letter patterns to represent sound patterns and writes them down (Steps 4 and 5). We must assume, also, that Jack is performing Step 6 correctly from his own point of view. The grapheme clumps "look right" to Jack. They represent what he intended them to represent. Also, he knows when he has finished; he can execute Step 7 correctly.

Now what about Sammy? Certainly Steps 1 and 2 are executed correctly. Sammy knows what he wants to say, and he knows what the words are supposed to sound like generally. Further, he has the *sounds* accurately segmented (Step 3). What he is not segmenting correctly are the letter patterns that represent those sounds (Step 4). Thus, we have the charming *boyleags* instead of *boiled eggs*. Of course we might wonder: does he *hear* the "ed" sound on *boiled*? Perhaps not. In that case, we would worry about a deficiency at Step 3. But in general, it appears that Sammy has less of a problem at the sound levels (Steps 2 and 3) than Jack does, and more of a problem at the grapheme level

(Steps 4 and 6). Sammy does not seem to have learned the correct orthographic representations of many of the word sounds in his head.

Now Peter. Read again Peter's second story, from which the words are taken. Are we sure Peter was choosing words accurately? Probably he was, but one can see from this why Step 1 has to be included in a model. The *idea* of attaching words to concepts is something the hearing population takes for granted. It cannot be taken for granted by teachers of the deaf. The deaf child must find other ways of conceptualizing objects and events —ways involving visual and motor representations. There are not enough words around, and words are not around *early* enough, for many deaf children to have become efficient in using them representationally. Does Peter have a similar problem? One at least thinks about that possibility in Peter's case, where one would never think about it in Sammy's case.

What about Step 2 for Peter? Does he grasp the overall sound frame of the word? Probably, although one cannot be sure in the case of *moeat* (money). With reference to Step 3, it does seem that Peter has tried to dissociate sound particles from the general sound stream, and that he has found some plausible associated letters (Step 4) that he can write down (Step 5). But disaster clearly strikes at Step 6—at least in the case of the words which were supposed to represent *coach* and *care.* The letters appear to have been put down any old way, and Peter seems to lack any awareness of the fact that only one way is proper. That is, he seems incapable of performing the test: "Does it look right?" at Step 6. Interestingly, however, he does seem to know that the word is finished. That is, he has an "enough" test that is separate from the "look right" test. Once he has put down "enough" letters, he is ready to quit.

Finally we come to Luke. Cheerful, creative Luke knows *exactly* what words he wants (Step 1), but that is about the end of it. In Luke's word list, we find many examples of implausible sound frames. Even in the case of his central character (the sark), which was repeatedly mentioned, Luke's graphemic rendition of "sark" is unconstrained by its overall sound frame. He does pay some attention to sound particles—the "k" sound, for instance, gets represented in "sakain," and the "g" sound gets represented in "grins." And from time to time, even some plausible letter patterns are put down (Steps 4 and 5), but Step 6 is (one presumes) hastily bypassed, and even Step 7 seems idiosyncratic. Like Peter, Luke appears to decide a word is finished simply because it has enough letters in it (or looks about the right length). He fails to consider whether or not the letters are in the right place, or even if they are the right letters (Step 6). Thus the heroic *throccatei* (helicopter).

The above analysis is only illustrative, and it is certainly not meant as an infallible guide. On the contrary, the point is that we do not need an infallible guide to begin getting a handle on the nature of a child's disability. We can use an informal program as a way of organizing some theoretical possibilities. These can then help us to organize some diagnostic and remedial possibilities.

About each of the four children, we would want to ask:

> Does he have the idea that more than one word can represent a concept?
>
> Does he have the correct overall sound pattern of a word he wants to use?
>
> Can he segment that pattern into sound particles, without losing the pattern?
>
> Does he know how the sound particles are represented graphemically? Does he have a stock of orthographically correct letter sets in semantic memory?
>
> Does writing them down cause him to forget the letters? The sounds?
>
> Can he match a set of visual letters in a memory set?
>
> Does he know that the matching operation is part of the task?
>
> Does he have a writing strategy of the form: "Put some letters down and hope for the best . . ."?

By thinking carefully about what learning-disabled children are actually doing—in addition to what we may think about their relationship to mothers and teachers, or about their emotional status, or about their general coping skills—we can make a highly effective start on designing new, individualized methods of diagnosis and remediation. That is the central message of information-processing psychology for teaching practice.

12/ "Two Right Hemispheres and None Left"

We have looked at some modern concepts of the human information-processing system, and reviewed research showing that
learning-disabled children may have processing difficulties with
certain stages of particular tasks. We then analyzed the reading
and spelling behavior of a few children, to illustrate how a general theoretical viewpoint can be applied to the individual case.
We are now ready to return to the issue of brain function, which,
as you will recall from the early chapters of the book, is how it
all began.

MODERN CONCEPTIONS OF HEMISPHERIC FUNCTIONS

The diagram in (5) schematizes the brain as it would look from
the top down. You can see the right and left hemispheres, the
eyes, and their connecting tracts. Assume they are in fact connected, that no brain damage has occurred. Now suppose you
are looking straight ahead, fixating on a central point several
feet in front of you. As the clear tracts show, everything you can
see (still staring straight ahead) in your left field of vision is being
seen by the right side of your brain. And, conversely, everything
in your right (shaded) field of vision is being seen by the left side
of your brain. The ears are also more strongly connected to opposite hemispheres. Sounds picked up by the right ear are mainly
registered by the left side of the brain; sounds picked up by the
left ear are registered by the right side of the brain.
The hands follow suit. The right hand is more strongly connected to the left hemisphere; the left hand, to the right hemi-

sphere. Normally, we move our eyes around and hear with both ears at about the same time. In addition, the two hemispheres themselves are connected by the *corpus callosum*. As long as all the callosal fibers are intact, the hemispheres can exchange information freely. That means both hemispheres are involved in processing the information picked up by the ears and eyes, but they are not necessarily involved in the same way. By testing one hemisphere at a time, scientists have learned that the hemispheres are specialized for certain types of cognition. This specialization is not yet fully understood, but the general picture is something like the following:

—The left hemisphere is specialized for language, and for serial processing.
—The right hemisphere is specialized for spatial and pictorial perception, and for wholistic processing.

It is important to understand that the specialized functions will appear in any task for which they are needed. Listening to music, for example, requires some serial processing (which the left hemisphere will handle) and some wholistic processing (the right hemisphere). An example of the latter is your recognition of the same tune being played in a different key. That instant of recognition, the matching up of the two melodic patterns, is wholistic in nature.

A so-called linear child on Werner's marble-board task is *not* a "left-hemispheric child," and the wholistic child is *not* a "right-hemispheric processor." Setting up a spatial objective—whether that objective is the last point of a line or a whole triangle—is a right-hemispheric function. Placing a marble is a left-hemispheric function, and so forth. The hemispheres always share in the work, although they may not share equally.

Reading and writing clearly involve both hemispheres. Words and letters, whether printed on a page or written by one's own hand, have spatial characteristics, for which the right hemisphere is specialized. Reading and writing also involve serial and language functions, for which the left hemisphere is specialized. In fluent reading and writing, the two hemispheres must coordinate their functions in intricate, high-speed sequential programs. We do not yet know exactly how this works. We do not have detailed models of reading and writing processes—which would be somewhat different for each of the many kinds of reading and writing tasks. The informal models shown in the last chapter are the merest sketches of what the real models will eventually include. But we can use them to illustrate the coordinated hemispheric interchange that must be going on. Consider the sounding-out task:

		Hemisphere
Step 1	Select a set of letters.	right
Step 2	Find their sounds.	left
Step 3	Articulate the sounds.	left
Step 4	Hold the sounds in working memory.	left
Step 5	Test: word finished?	right
Step 6	Integrate the sounds in working memory.	left
Step 7	Test: do I recognize the word?	left

The informal model of the writing task:

		Hemisphere
Step 1	Choose a word.	left
Step 2	Hold its overall sound in mind.	left
Step 3	Select a sound particle.	left
Step 4	Find a letter pattern in semantic memory.	right
Step 5	Write the letters.	left, for the motor action; right, for the configuration of the letters
Step 6	Test: do I recognize the letter pattern?	right
Step 7	Test: word finished?	right

You can see that it would make no sense to say that tasks of this sort are predominantly left-hemispheric or right-hemispheric. The theoretical situation is much more complicated than that: it involves a sequence of trade-offs between the hemispheres, a coordinated sharing of task requirements.

We come now to the question of disability. Where might the problem lie? There are at least three possibilities:

Problem 1—There may be a task-specific problem in moving information from one hemisphere to the other, essentially some kind of disconnection, perhaps of a few fibers of the corpus callosum or perhaps within one of the hemispheres. This may be why attentional deficits arise. The inability to switch one's attention systematically from Step 1 to Step 2, etc., of a task program may involve a physiological difficulty in switching control from one hemisphere to the other. The problem may not arise at the very beginning of a task, but only after fatigue effects have built up.

Problem 2—There may be a task-specific problem with one of the hemispheres, so that it performs inadequately when it takes its turn. Certain right-hemispheric deficiencies may characterize children with arithmetic disorders, for example. Suppose that every time the right hemisphere checked for the correct line-up of digits, a few critical brain cells "misfired." That could account for a child's failure to master—to the point of automaticity—the correct formatting rules for addition problems. If the rules never get into the format storehouse diagrammed in (30), then deficiencies would appear in particular working-memory programs that needed them.

Problem 3—There may be a task-specific problem of overall control by the left hemisphere. When we say that hemispheric switching occurs in a task, we must not lose sight of the fact that monitoring of the program as a whole must also occur. Where, in effect, does the program architect reside? What part of the brain assembles programs and makes sure they are running themselves off properly? As mentioned in Chapter 8, it is probably the case that this architect is verbal in nature. A telegraphic set of self-instructions, stored in the language areas of the brain, may govern the assembly and expression of working-memory programs. If something is wrong with the left hemisphere, then, a defect in "program control" may accompany Problem 2.

At this point in science, we do not have the technology to check out Problem 1. We have no way of tracking back-and-forth hemispheric activity during a multiple-step task like read-ing. Our technology is limited to the detection of gross hemi-spheric activities during the performance of very simple, single-step tasks. We cannot tell, even in those cases, exactly what a single hemisphere is doing; we can only tell that it is doing *some-thing* and that the other hemisphere is not. But that at least makes it possible for us to examine the likelihood that some ver-sion of Problem 2 and/or Problem 3 may be plausible.

There is an extensive literature on research of this type, and I will not attempt to review it here. Instead, I will concentrate on work from two laboratories—research that illuminates impor-tant portions of an emerging theoretical pattern.

STUDIES OF HEMISPHERIC DOMINANCE

First of all, it is necessary to understand the logic of *bilateral conflict* paradigms. As explained earlier, the following connec-tions are characteristic of normal human brains:

right hand
right visual field } connected to the left hemisphere
right ear

left hand
left visual field } connected to the right hemisphere
left ear

Suppose you heard (through earphones) one word in your left ear and another different word in your right ear. You heard both words at exactly the same time. Which word would you report first or most accurately? If you favor words coming into your right ear, we say that your left hemisphere has taken control of this task. If you favor words coming in through your left ear, we say that your right hemisphere has taken control.

Similarly, suppose we blindfold you and place two different objects in your hands. Which object would you identify most often and most accurately—the one in your left hand or the one in your right? Which hemisphere would take control of that task?

And, of course, the same thing can be done visually: two different patterns can be shown—one to your right field of vision and one to your left field. Which would you favor? Which hemisphere would take control?

Studies of this sort have suggested that certain simple tasks are routinely "grabbed" by one hemisphere or the other. This implies that the grabby hemisphere is specialized for handling tasks of that type. It is difficult to find a task that is a pure index of specialized right- or left-hemispheric skills, however. The following tasks are the best ones we have, and are now in use in many laboratories:

Modality	Type of stimulus material	Hemisphere
ears	digits, words, letters, syllables	left
ears	music, environmental sounds (dog barking, car horn, siren, etc.)	right
eyes	words, letters, digits	left
eyes	colors, forms (provided they are hard to name), dot patterns (same provision)	right
hands	letters, forms that are easy to name	left
hands	abstract forms (hard to name)	right

With this background, we are now ready to hear about research on dyslexic and normal children.

Witelson's contribution. Two publications with intriguing titles have appeared in *Science.* One was called "Sex and the Single Hemisphere," and the other, partly quoted as the title of the present chapter, was "Developmental Dyslexia: Two Right Hemispheres and None Left." Both articles, and other publications on similar topics, are by Sandra Witelson, a Canadian researcher affiliated with McMaster University.

Witelson invented the task described above for testing the hemispheric "controller" of handled objects—letters or abstract forms. She called it a *dichhaptic* task; *dich,* referring to the fact that stimuli were presented to both hands simultaneously, and *haptic*, referring to the handling modality.

She made two discoveries about this task: first, in males, the right hemisphere generally takes control of abstract haptic form recognition. This type of right-hemispheric dominance appears in males by the age of six. It does not, however, appear in females—as far as Witelson can tell, at least not by the age of fourteen, which was the oldest age group tested.[1] What this means is that females recognize abstract haptic forms with their left hemispheres as well as they do with their right hemispheres. Males recognize them better with their right hemispheres.

Except for dyslexic males. Males who cannot read behave like females who *can* read, on this particular task.[2]

What does it mean to have equally good left and right hemispheric skills on a "right-hemispheric type" task? It could mean one of two things: the left hemisphere may be able to do right-hemispheric processing—it may have, in effect, right-hemispheric skills; or (b) the left hemisphere may retain its own special skills, but it may try to do *everything* the left-hemispheric way. (Name the dichhaptic forms, for example.) Witelson believes that explanation (a) is the correct one for dyslexic males, which is why she subtitled her article "Two Right Hemispheres and None Left."[3] Explanation (b) may be the correct one for normally reading females.

What of dyslexic females? Dyslexic females (who are hard to find; Witelson could turn up only 15 as compared to 85 dyslexic males)—dyslexic females behave like normal females on the dichhaptic shapes task. We can only conclude that something else must be wrong with the dyslexic females.

As a matter of fact, something else *is* wrong with both the males and females who have reading disabilities. They also show deficient left-hemispheric processing on the dichotic listening task (digits). The left-hemispheric deficiency alone, apparently, is associated with dyslexia in females. But there are two problems for dyslexic males: the left hemisphere is not only deficient in its own skills, but it is also burdened with extra right-hemispheric skills. That may be why dyslexia is more frequent and often more severe in males than in females.

But the problem is even more complicated, according to a new team of researchers at the University of Wales.

Davidoff's contribution. Using a different right-hemispheric task—recognizing environmental sounds—J. B. Davidoff and his colleagues were surprised to discover that normal males switch to a *transitory* left-hemispheric dominance when their reading abilities reach the six-year-old level.[4] This finding is shown in (34) for two groups of children—middle-class and disadvan-

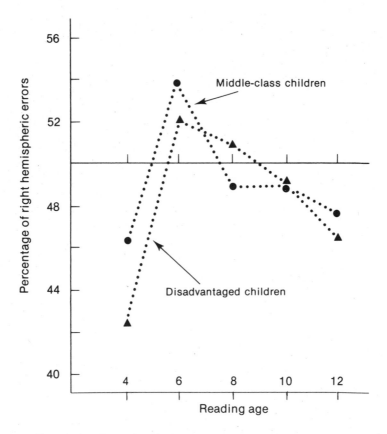

34. *Temporary loss of right-hemispheric control on environmental-sounds task. From Davidoff et al. (1978). Copyright 1978, Plenum. Reprinted by permission.*

taged. The graph shows that at the *reading* age of four, environmental sounds reported from the right hemisphere (heard by the left ear) are more often correct than sounds reported from the left hemisphere. But when reading age reached the six-year-old level, the left hemisphere became more accurate, temporarily.

Davidoff also tested his sample on a visual field task (dot patterns). On this task as well, males, but not females, switched from right- to left-hemispheric control—beginning at the reading age of six. This control peaked at the age of eight, and then dropped back. Normally, for males, the right hemisphere takes charge of that spatial task. We can see in (35) that the right hemisphere is generally more in charge for males than it is for females —who show no special changes with age, but who apparently handled the dot-detection task left-hemispherically all along.[5]

Davidoff has not yet tested dyslexics. But Davidoff's findings have the very important implication that reversals of hemispheric control may occur as a result of *learning sets* induced by reading instruction. Dyslexics probably have a reading age that is between six and eight, so their "two right hemispheres" may result from their efforts to learn how to read rather than from abnormality.

That is where the matter stands as we go to press. We know only five things for sure:

1. It is possible for one hemisphere to take control of a simple task that is presented—through the ears, eyes, or hands—to both hemispheres at once.
2. These dominance effects may change with development.
3. The effects may not be the same for males and females.
4. They may not be the same for dyslexic and normal children.
5. They may shift as a function of learning sets induced by certain forms of school instruction.

We will not really understand the significance of any of this for reading until a way is developed to encourage one hemisphere, rather than the other, to take control of particular stages of the reading process. At present we have no way of arranging that. To get a word, or any visual stimulus, into a single hemisphere, it must be flashed on and off before the eyes move—in less than 150 msec. In reading, because the eyes are moving down a line of

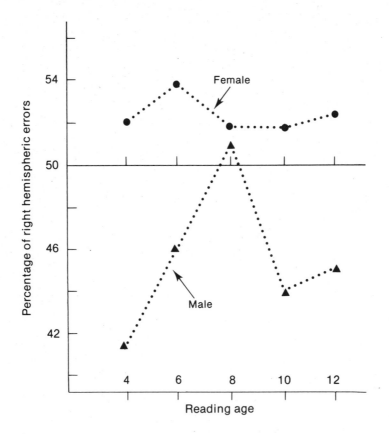

35. *Temporary loss of right-hemispheric control on dot-detection task —in males, not in females. From Davidoff et al. (1978). Copyright 1978, Plenum. Reprinted by permission.*

text, words are being picked up by both hemispheres at the same time. That may intensify hemispheric conflicts, and encourage the right hemisphere of some children to intrude inappropriately.

Suppose we could force the left hemisphere to do most of the work? Eran Zaidel, a biomedical engineering specialist at California Institute of Technology, is developing contact lenses that will screen out half the visual field, no matter which way the eyes are looking.[6] The technology is still cumbersome, and is not yet suitable for children, but improvements are being made. Within a few years, it should be possible to control the involvement of the hemispheres—at least to a greater degree than we can now—in the process of reading. Then we will be able to tell much more about how the brains of normal and dyslexic children actually work during reading and writing. For example, will normal children, forced to pick up a line of print with their right hemispheres, read like dyslexics? More hopefully, can we build up processing strength in the left hemispheres of dyslexic children? By making them (through contact lenses) pick up a line of print with the left hemisphere alone, we may be able to decrease the competition between the hemispheres, and the attempted "take over" of stages of the reading process by right-hemispheric strategies.

To test these possibilities, we must have a model of the reading process, something like the one described at the beginning of this chapter. We must have, in other words, a theory of how the left and right hemispheres are involved in the stages of processing the printed word. The theory in Chapter 9, the experiments in Chapter 10, and the models in Chapter 11—all these must be integrated with neuropsychological theories (like those in Chapter 12) about how the brain actually works. This is a very big job, but when that job is finally done we should understand what learning disabilities are, and we should be able to fix them.

References
Suggested Reading
Index

References

1 Compass Points

1. S. A. Kirk, in J. M. Kauffman and D. P. Hallahan, eds., *Teaching Children with Learning Disabilities: Personal Perspectives* (Columbus, Ohio: Merrill, 1976).
2. Federal Register, Vol. 41, no. 230, November 29, 1976. The definition was included in a proposed amendment published on that date. The amendment itself was substantially changed before being enacted into law early in 1978. The definition itself, however, remained unchanged.
3. W. M. Cruickshank, *The Brain-Injured Child in Home, School, and Community* (Syracuse: Syracuse University Press, 1967), p. 2.
4. L. J. Silverman and A. S. Metz, "Numbers of Pupils with Specific Learning Disabilities in Local Public Schools in the United States: Spring 1970," in F. F. de la Cruz, B. H. Fox, and R. H. Roberts, eds., *Minimal Brain Dysfunction* (New York: New York Academy of Sciences, 1973), p. 146.
5. The data are taken from the article by J. G. Minskoff, "Differential Approaches to Prevalence Estimates of Learning Disabilities," in F. F. de la Cruz, B. H. Fox, and R. H. Roberts, eds., *Minimal Brain Dysfunction* (New York: New York Academy of Sciences, 1973). The table includes: L. Eisenberg, "The Epidemiology of Reading Retardation and a Program of Preventive Intervention," in J. Money, ed., *The Disabled Reader* (Baltimore: Johns Hopkins Press, 1966). HEW National Advisory Committee on Dyslexia and Related Reading Disorders, *Reading Disorders in the United States* (Washington, D.C., 1969). H. R. Myklebust and B. Boshes, "Minimal Brain Damage in Children" (Final Report, United States Public Health Service Contract No. 108-65-142, 1969). R. Rubin and B. Balow, "Learning and Behavior Disorders: A Longitudinal Study," *Exceptional Children*, 1971, *38*, 293-299.

2 Early Views of the Brain-Injured Child

1. K. Goldstein, *Aftereffects of Brain Injuries in War* (New York: Grune & Stratton, 1942).
2. A. Strauss and L. S. Lehtinen, *Psychopathology and Education of the Brain-Injured Child* (New York: Grune & Stratton, 1947).
3. K. S. Lashley, *Brain Mechanisms and Intelligence* (New York: Dover, 1963).

4. J. J. McCarthy and Joan F. McCarthy, *Learning Disabilities* (Boston: Allyn and Bacon, 1963). The quotation, in a letter from Lehtinen, appears on p. 29.
5. H. G. Birch, ed., *Brain Damage in Children: The Biological and Social Aspects* (Baltimore: Williams & Wilkins, 1964), p. 6. Herbert Birch was first of all a very good experimental psychologist, a Ph.D. in physiological psychology. Later, he got a medical degree, specializing in pediatric neurology.
6. H. Werner, *Comparative Psychology of Mental Development* (New York: Science Editions, 1961; original copyright 1948).
7. All the quotations in this paragraph are from Werner, *Comparative Psychology of Mental Development*, p. 297.
8. D. Carrison and H. Werner, "Principles and Methods of Teaching Arithmetic to Mentally Retarded Children," *American Journal of Mental Deficiency*, 1943, 47, 309-317.
9. H. Werner, "Development of Visuo-Motor Performance on the Marble-Board Test in Mentally Retarded Children," *Journal of Genetic Psychology*, 1944, 64, 269-279.
10. A. A. Strauss and H. Werner, "Disorders of Conceptual Thinking in the Brain-Injured Child." *Journal of Nervous and Mental Disease*, 1942, 96, 153-172.
11. W. M. Cruickshank, *The Brain-Injured Child in Home, School and Community* (Syracuse: Syracuse University Press, 1967). W. M. Cruickshank, in J. M. Kauffman and D. P. Hallahan, eds., *Teaching Children with Learning Disabilities: Personal Perspectives* (Columbus: Merrill, 1976). N. C. Kephart, *The Slow Learner in the Classroom* (Columbus: Merrill, 1960).

3 Structural Approaches to Dyslexia

1. M. Critchley, *The Dyslexic Child* (London: Heinemann, 1970).
2. J. Hinshelwood, *Congenital Word-Blindness* (London: Lewis, 1917).
3. J. Hinshelwood, "A Case of Dyslexia: A Peculiar Form of Word-Blindness," *Lancet*, 1896, 2, 1451-1454.
4. Hinshelwood, "A Case of Dyslexia," 1453.
5. J. Hinshelwood, "A Case of 'Word' Without 'Letter' Blindness," *Lancet*, 1898, 1, 422-425.
6. J. Kerr, "School Hygiene, in its Mental, Moral and Physical Aspects," Howard Medal Prize Essay, *Journal of the Royal Statistical Society*, 1897, 60, 613-680.
7. J. Hinshelwood, "Word-Blindness and Visual Memory," *Lancet*, 1895, 2, 1564-1570.

8. W. Pringle Morgan, "A Case of Congenital Word-Blindness," *British Medical Journal*, 1896, 2, 1378.
9. J. Hinshelwood, "The Visual Memory for Words and Figures," *British Medical Journal*, 1896, 2, 1543-1544.
10. Hinshelwood, *Congenital Word-Blindness*, pp. 49-51.
11. J. Hinshelwood, " 'Letter' Without 'Word' Blindness," *Lancet*, 1899, 1, 83.
12. Hinshelwood, " 'Letter' Without 'Word'," p. 86.
13. Hinshelwood, *Congenital Word-Blindness*, pp. 53-55.
14. Hinshelwood, *Congenital Word-Blindness*, pp. 56-57.
15. N. Geschwind, *Selected Papers on Language and the Brain* (Boston: Reidel, 1976).

4 Functional Approaches to Dyslexia

1. S. T. Orton, " 'Word-Blindness' in School Children," *Archives of Neurology and Psychiatry*, 1925, 14, 582-615.
2. S. T. Orton, *Reading, Writing, and Speech Problems in Children* (New York: Norton, 1937).
3. Orton, "Word-Blindness," pp. 607, 608.
4. Although speech and motor disorders are included in some current definitions of learning disabilities, I have excluded them from this book on the same grounds that I have excluded discussions of blindness, retardation, physical disabilities (cerebral palsy) and psychosis. Extensive lines of theory and research on these disorders already exist and can be accessed by interested readers. The phenomena of disabled learning which *cannot* be tied to those other disorders form my subject.
5. A. Gillingham and B. Stillman, *Remedial Work for Reading, Spelling, and Penmanship* (New York: Sachette and Wilhems, 1940).
6. Gillingham and Stillman, *Remedial Work*, pp. 40-41.
7. J. L. Wiederholt, "Historical Perspectives in the Education of the Learning Disabled," in L. Mann and D. Sabatino, eds., *The Second Review of Special Education* (Philadelphia: Journal of Special Education Press, 1974).

5 Who Are the Learning-Disabled Children?

1. F. W. Owen, P. A. Adams, T. Forrest, L. M. Stolz, and S. Fisher, "Learning Disorders in Children: Sibling Studies," *Monographs of the Society for Research in Child Development*, 1971, Serial No. 144.
2. Owen et al., "Learning Disorders," p. 26.

3. Owen et al., "Learning Disorders," p. 31.
4. H. G. Birch and L. Belmont, "Auditory-Visual Integration in Normal and Retarded Readers," *American Journal of Orthopsychiatry*, 1964, *34*, 852-861.
5. Owen et al., "Learning Disorders," p. 36.
6. E. R. John et al., "Neurometrics," *Science*, 1977, *196*, 1393-1410.
7. Owen et al., "Learning Disorders," pp. 43, 44.

7 Arithmetic Disability

1. A. R. Luria, *Human Brain and Psychological Processes* (New York: Harper & Row, 1966), pp. 91-92. The classification of the disorders as Type I, Type II, etc., is my nomenclature, not Luria's.
2. A. R. Luria, *Higher Cortical Functions in Man* (New York: Basic Books, 1966), p. 160.
3. R. Cohn, "Arithmetic and Learning Disabilities," in H. R. Mykelbust, ed., *Progress in Learning Disabilities*, II (New York: Grune & Stratton, 1971).
4. Luria, *Human Brain*, p. 422.
5. Luria, *Human Brain*, pp. 454-456.
6. Luria, *Human Brain*, p. 253.
7. Luria, *Human Brain*, pp. 254, 257.
8. Herbert Ginsburg, *Children's Arithmetic: The Learning Process* (New York: Van Nostrand, 1977), pp. 124-125.
9. Ginsburg, *Children's Arithmetic*, pp. 140-143.
10. N. Geschwind, "Developmental Gerstmann Syndrome," *Selected Papers on Language and the Brain* (Boston: Reidel, 1974).

8 Hyperactivity

1. D. M. Ross and S. A. Ross, *Hyperactivity: Research, Theory, Action* (New York: Wiley, 1976), p. 288.
2. Ross and Ross, *Hyperactivity*, pp. 41-43.
3. B. L. Borland and H. K. Heckman, "Hyperactive Boys and Their Brothers," *Archives of General Psychiatry*, 1976, *33*, 669-675.
4. L. A. Sroufe, "Drug Treatment of Children with Behavior Problems," in F. D. Horowitz, ed., *Review of Child Development Research*, IV (Chicago: University of Chicago Press, 1975).
5. Ross and Ross, *Hyperactivity*, pp. 165-166.
6. L. Beck, W. S. Langford, M. MacKay, and G. Sum, "Childhood Chemotherapy and Later Drug Abuse and Growth Curve: A Follow-Up Study of 30 Adolescents," *American Journal of Psychiatry*, 1975, *132*, 436-438. L. Eisenberg, "The Hyperkinetic Child and Stimulant Drugs," *New England Journal of Medicine*, 1972, *287*,

249-250. D. J. Safer, R. P. Allen, and E. Barr, "Depression of Growth in Hyperactive Children on Stimulant Drugs," *New England Journal of Medicine*, 1972, *287*, 217-220. D. J. Safer, R. P. Allen, and E. Barr, "Growth Rebound after Termination of Stimulant Drugs," *Journal of Pediatrics*, 1975, *86*, 113-116.

7. J. M. Tanner, *Education and Physical Growth* (New York: International Universities Press, 1970).
8. G. R. Newell and B. E. Henderson, "Case-Control Study of Hodgkin's Disease. I. Results of the Interview Questionnaire," *Journal of the National Cancer Institute*, 1973, *51*, 1437-1441.
9. J. M. Swanson and M. Kinsbourne, "Stimulant-Related State Dependent Learning in Hyperactive Children," *Science*, 1976, *192*, 1354-1357.
10. H. J. van Duyne, "Effects of Stimulant Drug Therapy on Learning Behavior in Hyperactive/MBD Children," in R. M. Knights and D. J. Bakker, eds., *The Neuropsychology of Learning Disorders* (Baltimore: University Park Press, 1976).
11. Ross and Ross, *Hyperactivity*, pp. 146-228.
12. S. W. Porges, G. F. Walter, R. J. Korb, and R. L. Sprague, "The Influences of Methylphenidate on Heart Rate and Behavioral Measures of Attention in Hyperactive Children," *Child Development*, 1975, *46*, 727-733.
13. D. Meichenbaum, "Self-Instructional Methods," in F. Kanfer and A. Goldstein, eds., *Helping People Change* (New York: Pergamon Press, 1975), pp. 384-385.
14. A recent issue of *Science*, 1978, vol. 199, no. 4328, contains an excellent summary and two new research reports, updating scientific and governmental positions on hyperactivity and stimulant drugs.

9 The Information-Processing Approach

1. The references under Cognitive Science and Reading, in the Suggested Reading section at the end of this book, will provide an introduction to the area. A more detailed bibliography is available in S. Farnham-Diggory, "The Cognitive Point of View," in D. J. Treffinger, J. K. Davis, and R. E. Ripple, eds., *Handbook on Teaching Educational Psychology* (New York: Academic Press, 1977).
2. The quotation is from D. W. Massaro and D. Klitzke, "Letters are Functional in Word Identification," *Memory and Cognition*, 1977, *5*, 292-298. Massaro's review of letter and word recognition in reading is in D. W. Massaro, ed., *Understanding Language: An Information Processing Analysis of Speech Perception, Reading, and Psycholinguistics* (New York: Academic Press, 1975).
3. A paper by Moscovitch reviews modern work that is relevant to

one of Orton's basic points: either hemisphere can handle early stages of processing, but hemispheric specialization appears at later stages of processing. M. Moscovitch, "Using Peripheral and Central Masking To Infer the Locus at Which Perceptual and Hemispheric Asymmetries Emerge," in M. S. Gazzaniga, ed., *The Handbook of Neurobiology: Volume on Neuropsychology* (New York: Plenum Press, forthcoming).

10 Information-Processing in Dyslexia

1. In five-year-olds, a letter can be masked at 125 msec, which means it is not fully registered even by then. In eight-year-olds and ten-year-olds, a letter can be masked at 75 msec. Not until the age of twelve or thirteen is the 50-msec registration time achieved. See the following: P. H. Liss and M. M. Haith, "The Speed of Visual Processing in Child and Adults—Effects of Backward and Forward Masking," *Perception and Psychophysics*, 1970, *8*, 396-398. R. F. Welsandt and P. A. Meyer, "Visual Masking, Mental Age, and Retardation," *Journal of Experimental Child Psychology*, 1974, *18*, 512-519. R. F. Welsandt, J. J. Zupnick, and P. A. Meyer, "Age Effects in Backward Visual Masking," *Journal of Experimental Child Psychology*, 1973, *15*, 454-461.
2. G. Stanley and R. Hall, "Short-Term Visual Information Processing in Dyslexics," *Child Development*, 1973, *44*, 841-844. Also see G. Stanley and R. Hall, "A Comparison of Dyslexics and Normals in Recalling Letter Arrays After Brief Presentations," *British Journal of Educational Psychology*, 1973, *43*, 301-304.
3. C. K. Conners, K. Kramer, and F. Guerra, "Auditory Synthesis and Dichotic Listening in Children with Learning Disabilities," *Journal of Special Education*, 1969, *3*, 163-170.
4. P. Tallal, "Implications of Speech Perceptual Research for Clinical Populations," in J. Kavanaugh and J. Jenkins, eds., *Language Research in the Laboratory, Clinic, and Classroom*, in press.
5. A. S. Reger and D. L. Scarborough, *Toward a Psychology of Reading*, (Hillsdale: Erlbaum, 1977).
6. F. J. Morrison, B. Giordani, J. Nagy, "Reading Disability: An Information-Processing Analysis," *Science*, 1977, *196*, 77-79.
7. C. Spring and C. Capps, "Encoding Speed, Rehearsal, and Probed Recall of Dyslexic Boys," *Journal of Educational Psychology*, 1974, *66*, 780-786.
8. Geschwind (see Chapters 3 and 8) has reported a case of color-naming failure associated with the loss of reading ability. N. Geschwind, "Color-Naming Defects in Association with Alexia," *Selected Papers on Language and the Brain* (Boston: Reidel, 1976).

9. Three other recent experiments report a similar primacy defect and a similar rehearsal defect: H. L. Swanson, "Nonverbal Visual Short-Term Memory as a Function of Age and Dimensionality in Learning Disabled Children," *Child Development*, 1977, *48*, 51-55. J. Torgesen and T. Goldman, "Verbal Rehearsal and Short-Term Memory in Reading Disabled Children," *Child Development*, 1977, *48*, 56-60. R. H. Bauer, "Memory Processes in Child with Learning Disabilities: Evidence for Deficient Rehearsal," *Journal of Experimental Child Psychology*, 1977, *24*, 415-430.
10. S. Farnham-Diggory and L. W. Gregg, "Short Term Memory Function in Young Readers," *Journal of Experimental Child Psychology*, 1975, *19*, 279-298.

12 *"Two Right Hemispheres and None Left"*

1. S. Witelson, "Sex and the Single Hemisphere: Specialization of the Right Hemisphere for Spatial Processing," *Science*, 1976, *193*, 425-427.
2. S. Witelson, "Neural and Cognitive Correlates of Developmental Dyslexia: Age and Sex Differences," in C. Shagass, S. Gershon, and A. Friedhoff, eds., *Psychopathology and Brain Dysfunction* (New York: Raven Press, 1977). Two recent reports, which were independent of Witelson's, came to similar conclusions. J. R. Kershner, "Cerebral Dominance in Disabled Readers, Good Readers, and Gifted Children: Search for a Valid Model," *Child Development*, 1977, *48*, 61-67, wrote: "[Since] results reflect a greater participation of right-hemisphere-based perceptual processes in poor readers . . . reading disability may be the result of a perceptual coding strategy . . . that is inappropriate to the processing demands . . . and inefficient for the achievement of academic success." B. Guyer and M. Friedman, "Hemispheric Processing and Cognitive Styles in Learning Disabled and Normal Children," *Child Development*, 1975, *46*, 658-668, concluded: "Learning-disabled [children] perform as well as the control group on right-hemispheric tasks . . . The cognitive processing abilities that were deficient in learning-disabled children can all be theoretically related to left . . . hemisphere functioning . . . Learning-disabled children may be attempting to use a nonverbal information processing mode [a right-hemispheric style] to deal with academic tasks."
3. S. Witelson, "Developmental Dyslexia: Two Right Hemispheres and None Left," *Science*, 1977, *195*, 309-311.
4. J. B. Davidoff, B. P. Cone, and J. P. Scully, "Developmental Changes in Hemispheric Processing for Cognitive Skills and the Relationship to Reading Ability," in A. M. Lesgold, J. W. Pellegrino,

S. Fokkema, and R. Glaser, eds., *Cognitive Psychology and Instruction* (New York: Plenum, 1978).

5. Davidoff et al. have plotted the proportion of left-ear errors to total errors. That is the same thing as the proportion of right-hemispheric errors. I have relabeled the ordinates accordingly.

6. E. Zaidel, "A Technique for Presenting Lateralized Visual Input with Prolonged Exposure," *Vision Research*, 1975, 15, 283-289.

Suggested Reading

LEARNING DISABILITY AND DYSLEXIA

MacDonald Critchley, *The Dyslexic Child* (London: Heinemann, 1970). Critchley is by all odds the most authoritative and interesting medical scholar of dyslexia. This collection of his papers includes a number of literary examples (e.g., from Dickens) of dyslexia.

F. de la Cruz, B. H. Fox, and R. H. Roberts, eds., *Minimal Brain Dysfunction* (Annals of the New York Academy of Sciences, Vol. 205, 1973). A good source of general information, sampling medical, educational, and psychological opinion.

J. M. Kauffman and D. P. Hallahan, eds., *Teaching Children with Learning Disabilities: Personal Perspectives* (Columbus, Ohio: Merrill, 1976). Informal summary, comments, and personal history from many of the founding fathers of the field, such as Cruickshank and Samuel Kirk (who developed the Illinois Test of Psycholinguistic Abilities). Interesting reading and gives a more accurate picture of what they intended their "schools" to do than is given by some of their followers.

R. M. Knights and D. J. Bakker, eds., *The Neuropsychology of Learning Disorders* (Baltimore: University Park Press, 1976). An excellent collection of readings, far and away the best of the many available collections.

J. J. McCarthy and J. F. McCarthy, *Learning Disabilities* (New York: Allyn, 1969). A paperback text that is somewhat old but gives a good summary of the state of the art in learning-disabilities courses.

D. M. Ross and S. A. Ross, *Hyperactivity: Research, Theory, Action* (New York: Wiley, 1976). An excellent review of the field by two psychologists with clinical hearts and experimental minds. It lays out the history of the problem, statistics, facts, treatment alternatives, and it tries to show what hyperactivity means from the standpoint of the child.

BRAIN DAMAGE

Norman Geschwind, *Selected Papers on Language and the Brain* (Boston: Reidel, 1976). A collection of fascinating papers by our foremost clinical neurologist, who is also an authority on the historical foundations of his field. He writes with clarity and charm, and makes comprehensible the logic, as well as the intricacies, of neurological research.

Marcel Kinsbourne, "Cognitive Deficit: Experimental Analysis," in J. L. McGauge, ed., *Psychobiology* (New York: Academic Press, 1971). A good review of how to utilize information-processing concepts in the assessment of brain damage.

M. D. Lezak, *Neuropsychological Assessment* (New York: Oxford University Press, 1976). A handbook of psychometric procedures which can be used in studying brain-damaged adults and children.

COGNITIVE SCIENCE AND READING

R. B. Eisenberg, *Auditory Competence in Early Life* (Baltimore: University Park Press, 1975). This may tell you more than you wanted to know about infant perception, but it also provides good summaries and organizing principles for the field of auditory perceptual development.

R. N. Haber and M. Hershenson, *The Psychology of Visual Perception* (New York: Holt, 1973). This is the textbook on the physiological and psychological processes of perception that I like the best, of the many on the market.

J. F. Kavanaugh and I. G. Mattingly, eds., *Language by Ear and by Eye* (Cambridge: MIT Press, 1972). One of the earliest and best collections of the work of basic cognitive researchers writing about the applications of their work to an understanding of processes involved in reading and writing.

Peter Lindsay and Donald Norman, *Human Information Processing* (New York: Academic Press, 1977). The classic, best-selling text in the area.

D. W. Massaro, ed., *Understanding Language: An Information Processing Analysis of Speech Perception, Reading, and Psycholinguistics* (New York: Academic Press, 1975). A collection of papers primarily from Massaro's laboratory. They show you how an elegant information-processing psychologist thinks, and Massaro is one of the best.

A. S. Reber and D. L. Scarborough, *Toward a Psychology of Reading* (Hillsdale: Erlbaum, 1977). Somewhat more recent than the Kavanaugh and Mattingly collection, this one also includes a massive review by Gleitman and Rozin of reading research.

Index

Left hemisphere: Orton on function of, 27-30, 94; failures in control by, 30-32; and sequence, 42; specialization of, 126; coordination with right, 126-128; dominance by, 128. *See also* Strephosymbolia
Lehtinen, Laura, 9
Logic, defects of, 65-66
Luria, A. R., 64-70, 72, 73

Marble-board test, 12, 34, 93, 126
Masking, perceptual, 98-102; factors in, 99-100
Massaro, D. W., 93-94
Meaning, 88-90; and the semantic network, 89
Medical history, of learning-disabled children, 43
Meichenbaum, Donald, 84-86, 92
Memory, visual: Hinshelwood on, 17; semantic, 90; working, 90; impairment of, and dyslexia, 102-105; tests of span of, 108
Memory scanning, 108, 112-113; auditory vs. visual, 113
Methylphenidate (Ritalin), 78, 81, 82-83
Mirror writing, 27
Morgan, Pringle, 19, 75
Morrison, F. J., 102-105
Mothers, of learning-disabled children, 45-46
Motor aphasia, developmental, 31

Naming, ability in. *See* Semantic network
National Association for Children with Learning Disabilities, 3
Neurological assessment of learning-disabled children, 42-43

Orton, S. T., 1, 8, 34, 42; on word blindness, 27-32; on theory of reading, 28-30; on strephosym-

bolia, 30-32; on remedial training, 32-33; and information processing, 94
Owen, Freya, 35-46

Parents, attitudes of toward learning-disabled child, 44-46
Perception, Werner on, 12
Perceptual masking, in reading, 98-102
Perceptual-motor skills, and learning disability, 40-42
Perceptual synthesis, 88
Piaget, Jean, 93
Planning, defects in, 66-67
Porges, Stephen, 81-83, 92, 96
Primacy effect, in memory, 107
Programs, in memory, 90; example of, 90-91; of the learning-disabled child, 94-95
Protocol analysis, 114; vs. task analysis, 114-115; examples of, 115-124
Psychometric instruments for data on learning disabilities, 35-46
Psychopathology and Education of the Brain-injured Child (Strauss and Lehtinen), 9

Reading: theories of normal and defective, 22-26; Orton on, 28-30. *See also* Dyslexia
Reading aloud, and perceptual masking, 100
Reading, Writing, and Speech Problems in Children (Orton), 27
Recency effect, in memory, 107
Rehearsal skills, of dyslexic children, 107
Responsiveness to stimuli, forced, 13-14
Right hemisphere, 126; coordination with left, 126-128; and sex differences, 131-134